Part of The Abundance Plan Book Series

Make Your Money Work for You

Level Up Your Finances with New Mindsets, Planning, Habits and Goals

By Krista Dunk

Make Your Money Work for You
© 2019 by Krista Dunk
www.SaveMoneyandBuildWealth.com

This title is also available in Kindle format.

Published by 100X Publishing
Vacaville, CA
www.100Xacademy.com

All rights reserved. No part of this publication may be reproduced, stored in a retrieval system, or transmitted in any form or by any means--for example, electronic, photocopy, recording--without the prior written permission of the publisher.
Scripture taken from the New King James Version®. Copyright © 1982 by Thomas Nelson. Used by permission. All rights reserved.

ISBN: 9-781-6920-7209-4

Printed in the United States of America

With contribution by Chris Creekpaum

Dedication

To God, through whom all things are possible.

To my family, Chris, Christian, Karissa and my parents and siblings, for whom I am very thankful.

To the reader, who I pray will have a revelation that where they are now is not where they have to stay.

Table of Contents

Introduction ……7

Chapter 1: Mindsets and Habits ……10

Chapter 2: Spending Habits ……22

Chapter 3: Self-Control ……40

Chapter 4: Bye-Bye Debt ……46

Chapter 5: Setting Goals for Your Financial Future ……59

Chapter 6: Investing ……70

Chapter 7: Retirement ……82

Chapter 8: Legacy ……91

Conclusion ……109

Resources Section ……113

About the Author ……115

Speaking and Training ……116

Introduction

Money isn't everything, as they say. But, money is something…something we all need.

The current state of your finances might be terrible, poor, okay, pretty good, or maybe even great. No matter where you are now, there is a next level for you; a next step up. A majority of what it will take to get from here to there involves new thinking and new habits.

Awareness (knowledge) → **Vision** (understanding) → **Wise Action** (wisdom)

Money may not solve all of life's problems, but it can certainly solve every money problem! You've probably heard the saying: we don't know what we don't know. When it comes to money, this is especially true. Some of us grew up with wealthy parents, learning their money habits, strategies and mindsets. Most of us didn't. *They know something I don't*, we often think about people with money. But, guess what? We can learn!

As we begin, we want to note that there's a typical progression to a person's financial education and financial life. Where are you at today?

Poverty/Survival	Building
Struggle	Abundance
Getting By	Financial Freedom
Stability	Generational Wealth

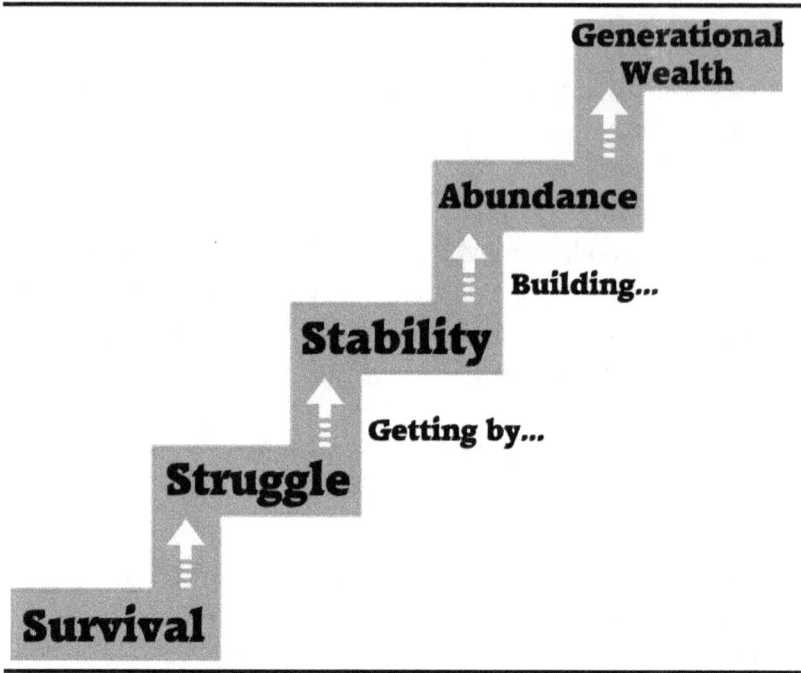

At every step, to reach the next level requires new knowledge, a new thought process and upgraded habits. Some transitions from step to step are easier than others. To make the transition from struggle to getting by might be as simple as getting a new job with better pay. But, even that transition will involve some new habits and knowledge. Some steps up, such as abundance to generational wealth, are more challenging, necessitating an uncomfortable shift or a longer timeframe, education and training, and most certainly a new self-image (mindset).

Interestingly, who we are inside (at our core – our hearts, motives, belief systems, etc.) has a huge impact on our finances. It took me a long time to realize this truth.

Money is a tool. It's time to learn how to be skilled with using it. Read on and learn how to develop your mindset and habits, which will then help you reach the next step up, enlarge your wallet and make the world a better place.

Our prayer and hope is that you take the tips, ideas and information in this book (and other books in this series) and run with it. Our goal is to teach for transformation, not just information. Information is great, but transformation makes a lasting change, even for future generations of your family.

>*"Transformation is a byproduct of application."*
>—Pedro Adao

After reading this, if you need more help and coaching, please visit our website and Facebook page to find out when our next online Save Money and Build Wealth Financial Coaching classes are happening. These classes will give you the opportunity to ask specific questions and to have a community of others taking the same journey to Save Money and Build Wealth.

www.SaveMoneyandBuildWealth.com
www.facebook.com/groups/savemoneyandbuildwealth

Ready to start this journey?

Chapter 1

Mindsets and Habits

As I already mentioned, every one of us has a next step for our financial journey if we choose to take it. Whatever it is, it will require us to have new knowledge, mindsets and habits to reach and sustain that new level. For anyone whose finances are in the terrible, poor or okay (ish) levels right now, challenging decisions may be required! Our current ways of thinking got us where we are today, but there is hope! We can learn new things.

"We don't know what we don't know."

Although it might be uncomfortable, endure the pain for a time, knowing the promise of better financial days are coming. This season of hyper focus on taking control of your spending habits, setting a budget, getting creative and finding solutions, learning self-control, setting goals, paying down debt, or whatever area needs work is temporary.

It's like going on a money diet. The strict diet shouldn't last forever, but hopefully should produce new habits and gets you noticeable results. Why do people go on diets in the first place? It's because they envision something different for themselves. They're most likely unhappy with the current state of their health and size. They realize something has gone wrong and they need a reset. The extra weight has become heavy, physically and emotionally. If you think about it, the weight of financial problems isn't much different.

Maybe you're not in debt right now or struggling much with your finances. Maybe you aren't spending more than you make or living paycheck to paycheck. Even in that case there may be a nagging feeling of knowing there's a next level...somewhere. You could be a better steward of your money, but you just aren't sure what to do. How to find financial freedom seems elusive. Whenever you want to go to the next level, you need to first recognize where you're at.

Just for fun, we've created some money personas – a few characters who have common money issues (who may or may not be based on actual people we've known...).

Money Personas

First is Doris the Diva. Doris is *image poor*, meaning in order to keep up her image and looks, Doris is spending a fortune every month, unable to save anything. She's living paycheck to paycheck, mostly because her monthly spending on nails, hair services and products, makeup, shoes, new clothing, jewelry, and other beauty treatments is spectacularly high. She has a small, lackluster apartment and a sporty little car (with a car payment of course). Doris the Diva doesn't make a lot of money, but she certainly wants to look like she's perfect when she's out and about. Doris is *image poor*.

Doris the Diva's aunt, Auntie Diamond, is an older, richer version of her. Auntie Diamond has some money and wants everyone to know it. Like Doris, her image and looks are top priority. Unlike Doris though, Auntie Diamond can afford it. Or at least for now. Auntie Diamond doesn't have a lot of meaningful relationships or a sense of purpose, so she tries to fill the void and find a sense of value through things. Auntie

Diamond is *poor in purpose.*

Then there's Steve the Spender. Steve has just about every big-boy toy you can think of: motorcycle, ATV, boat, upscale vehicles, tools galore, every electronic device you can think of, a pool, etc., and the insurance and loan payments to go with. Unfortunately, this has made Steve *stuff poor.* His stuff is making him poor. He makes good money, because he works really hard…to pay for all his stuff. And regrettably, because he works so much to pay for his stuff, he doesn't have much time to spend using all his toys. Steve spends nearly all of his paycheck on stuff payments and hasn't been able to save effectively. He feels proud of his pile of stuff, although the debt pile is also growing, and he's not sure he can retire. But, everyone always wants to head over to Steve's for a party…if he is ever home. Steve is *stuff poor.*

Stagnant Stella is next. Stella is doing okay financially, but she's stuck. She doesn't have any strategies for growing her money. She has a good job and mostly good spending habits, and even has some money stashed away in her savings account. Stella's modest, but good-quality car is paid off and she enjoys traveling with friends and family from time to time. In her mind, she knows there has to be more—more she could be doing, more investments available, more growth strategies—but she doesn't have the knowledge and doesn't want to make a bad financial decision, so she's done nothing. Stella is *poor in strategy.*

Miser Matt lives a small life. While it can be wise to be frugal, Miser Matt takes it to the extreme. Matt has a huge amount of money in his savings account, but no one would ever know it. Fear keeps him hoarding his huge account.

He's not generous, he won't invest in anything, he has many fears about the world's economy, his mindset is focused on scarcity, and he won't even buy himself a pair of new shoes when he needs it. Although Matt appears wealthy on his bank statement, his mindset is not. He is *poor in mindset*.

Lastly, there's Ebony and Ivory. They're a couple who cannot agree about money – how, when, why, where, or what to spend it on. Ebony grew up in a home where her parents spent money freely, buying whatever, whenever, even if it meant getting personal loans, lines of credit or racking up credit card debt to do so. Ivory grew up seeing his parents calculating and analyzing every purchase and every dollar spent, in a more tight-fisted environment. Ebony and Ivory hardly know how to communicate with each other when it comes to money, because their perspectives are so different. Ebony and Ivory are *poor in agreement and joint vision*.

Can you relate to any of these people? Do any of their situations sound familiar?

> *"Too many people spend money they earned, to buy things they don't want, to impress people that they don't like."*
> –Will Rogers

What's Your Money Story?

Growing up, we all formulated some kind of "money story," most likely subconsciously. Not many of us have had parents who've taken purposeful time to teach us all the ins and outs of the financial world. Many of our parents were just doing their best based on the small amount of information they had to work with. Ah, if only to have been born a Rockefeller, a

Hilton or a Gates!

But, we all learned at least a thing or two, right? What we observed and were taught in our family of origin (either directly/intentionally or subconsciously) started to write a money story in our minds. Here's what I learned (Krista):

My first memories are of our small house on half an acre at the end of a dead-end street. We grew a garden each spring and summer, my dad had a stash of firewood for the fireplace in a shed he built in the yard My dad also had a steady stream of different cars he would buy, fix and resell while working his full-time teaching job. My mom was a substitute teacher who often sewed clothing items for my younger sister and I. Looking back, we didn't have much, and I've since been told that many of my clothes were from the Salvation Army.

As I grew up, my parents divorced just as I was going into Jr. High. Just prior to that, I remember thinking we were finally starting to have some money. Our family got a new car, the answer wasn't always "no" to requests for that popular sweatshirt all the kids had or those shoes, or…

After the divorce, our lack of money seemed painfully obvious for a while. We never went hungry or even close, but mainly I remember noticing the difference between what I had and was able to do vs. my friends. At age 16, I got my first job and continued working until my first child was born when I was 28.

My money story became don't spend money, stash it all away in a savings account, work hard, get a practical safe job, be responsible with payments and bills, and having a lot of money is unnecessary and greedy.

My husband, Chris, had a slightly different experience growing up. He grew up in a military family and lived on several military bases. Somehow his mom made their household's budget work. She was a master at stretching and maximizing every dollar his dad's soldier pay provided. She, like my mom, would sew clothing for everyone in their family and even other things like bedding, kitchen towels and decorative items.

In his quest to have his own video game, book, bike and candy money, Chris had various jobs even as a kid (mowing lawns, paper route, etc.). He learned the power of hard work early on and even to this day is one of the hardest working, diligent people I know.

His money story and mine ended up being similar in some ways, which, I might add, helps us to be in agreement much of the time when it comes to money discussion and plans. He learned extreme frugality, if you had any money you should save it, and that wasting anything was bad.

Chris the Save Money Maven had a money story too. Her money story started in church. Here's her story, in her own words:

"In my room I had a bank in which I was taught to put a small portion of my money into. When money was in there, I was proud to drop it in the offering plate the next Sunday. Giving made me proud and happy.

As I grew up, I never really contemplated whether we were

poor or not. My parents never openly talked about money in front of us kids. We always had food in the fridge and my grandma made us new pajamas every Christmas. We got a gift on our birthdays and a couple gifts, usually clothes or something we needed and one thing we had wished for, at Christmas. We lived in (what I considered) pretty houses, but it turns out my mom was just a great housekeeper and homemaker. My dad always had our yard mowed and trimmed, and looking back, I figure he must have worked hard on repairs. Wherever we lived the houses were tidy and fixed up.

I remember being taught that I had to work for "extras." My parents would spend a certain amount of money on my school clothes, but if I wanted more (and what girl didn't) I had to buy it myself. So, I babysat, picked fruit and mowed yards to earn money for shoes and clothes, make up and entertainment. I wasn't ever really taught to save, but I usually had a few bucks hidden away. I'm embarrassed to say that I kept part of my allowance hidden away to loan to my brother later, for a high-interest-rate loan. Sorry, Ron!

In junior high, I remember a friend saying she couldn't hang out that evening because it was payday and her family was going shopping. I was so confused. Did everyone get paid today? Why didn't I get money today? Did my parents get money today? Who was it from? That was the day I realized that my friend's family didn't have much in the way of groceries the week before this mysterious "payday." I always had food. Our power was never shut off and we always had a phone. Later I realized my friend's mom stayed home with the kids and the dad only got paid once a month, so it was a family fun night. I never knew when my parents got paid, because I always had what I wanted and/or needed. My mom always had me grocery shop with her on the weekend, so I didn't think that was fun at all. I couldn't believe my friend thought going grocery shopping was fun!

Indirectly I learned a few things about money from my parents, but nothing directly. No money training, no money conversations. Looking back, there was one clue that I should have realized. My dad would get all the envelopes (bills) and lay them out on the living room floor. He would spend long periods of time rearranging them and writing on the envelopes. He wrote things on them like "check 1009, $104.30." I now know he was saying how and when he paid the bill. He was probably prioritizing them when he moved them around in their neat little rows. I watched him organizing, but wasn't sure what he was doing at the time.

I also remember my dad coming home with cars, trucks, a bedroom set and one time a one-carat (real) diamond ring. My mom was too afraid of getting mugged, so she would never wear it. I thought, why can't I have $10 to go to the movies with my friends if dad gets to buy a truck? It made no sense to me. Well, now I know that my dad traded and bartered frequently. He would take something in trade, fix it up and clean it up and resell it for more. That's why we didn't have $10, but we usually had an extra vehicle in the driveway.

As an adult, I'm not really great about saving money, I prefer to reinvest it and keep it "moving." I guess I get this from my dad. I also love buying, selling and trading. It makes me feel like I get to keep a little more of my paycheck than the other guy does. I've always worked a full-time job, paid all my bills on time and kept food in the fridge. I still love generosity and have had many money conversations with my young-adult daughter. What's the money story you are telling your kids? Is it a story of scarcity or abundance?"

Money stories just happen, but what if the money story we learned is holding us back? What if there's more, a *lot* more to the money story we need in order to be fruitful? I suspect some people's money story needs a complete re-write!

Abundance Mindset, Not Poverty Mindset

If you've read our book *Spiritual Principles of Money*, in it we talk a lot about the importance of a higher mindset. A new mindset is a must if we want anything different in life than what we have now. If you stay at your current level of understanding, you'll stay at your current level of finances (and relationships, health, career path, and…).

> *"I need to stop getting into situations where all my options are potentially bad."* –Jack Campbell, *Dauntless*

People who tend to have scarcity mindsets might have thoughts like these:

There isn't enough.
There's never enough.
I can't afford it.
If that person gets an opportunity, then there isn't one for me.
If they have money, it means less is available to me.
The future is going to be tough.
They owe me.
Thinking small keeps me safe.

I cannot be generous, because there won't be enough left for me.
Get all I can, when I can, and hoard it all.

Do you see the theme? Scarcity mindset is based in fear; fear of not enough paired with our selfish tendencies. Can you see how even people who have a lot of money can still have this poverty mindset? Wealthy and poor people alike with this mindset might be more apt to take advantage of others in order to get money.

What's interesting is how pervasive and sneaky it is. Many of us have grown up learning poverty thinking and it infiltrates our thoughts, beliefs and actions in ways we don't always recognize.

Abundance thinking/mindset doesn't come naturally and is the opposite of poverty mindset. Abundance mindset thinks thoughts like these:

There is enough.
I can be generous.
How can I afford it?
When I sow, I will reap.
Someone else's success is evidence that I can do it too.
I can be optimistic, think big and take calculated risks.
The best is yet to come.
I have control over my own future and success, and it's filled with possibility.
My more-than-enough flows out to help others.

This mindset is not fear based. It thinks higher. I'd be deceiving you if I said this mindset is something you can muster the will power to achieve. Not the case. The only way I've been able to change my default (and crappy) poverty-mindset thinking has been to renew my mind with what God says about money and His way of thinking. It's vastly different than our default, and the process of change takes a while…it's continuous, actually.

In his newsletter, *Rich Dad Poor Dad Daily*, author and real estate mogul, Robert Kiyosaki had this to say about abundance vs. scarcity thinking:

My poor dad would always say, "I can't afford that." My rich dad would counteract this sentiment with the question, "How can I afford that?" One way of thinking, the poor dad way, sees a world of scarcity. Even today there are people locked into the idea of treating their hard-earned money with a scarcity driven mindset. The other way of thinking sees a world of abundance. The problem with the phrase, "I can't afford that," is that it's a soul-killing phrase. There is no hope in a phrase like that. It kills dreams in an economy where it's more important than ever to dream big. Rather than say, "I can't afford that," I encourage you to begin thinking with a new money mindset and to being asking, "How can I afford it?" Asking that question is life-giving. There is hope in that question. Asking, "How can I afford it," allows you to dream as big as your desired goal.

To be clear, what I'm not saying is to spend money when you don't have it on liabilities. What I am saying is to begin thinking how you can make more money so that you can afford some of the fine things in life. I'm asking you to start thinking with a mindset of abundance rather than with a mindset of scarcity.

When we think differently, we can behave differently. With money, it's our actions that make the difference.

>Beliefs control thinking.
>Thinking controls actions.
>Actions become habits.
>Habits set our life's course.

Like a well-worn trail through the woods or field, habits are our daily path, whether the worn path leads us to a beautiful beach or a garbage dump. If you aren't satisfied with where your pathway keeps leading you, get off it and create a new one.

Chapter 2

Spending Habits

Chris and I got married in the early 90's when home loans were much more difficult to get for young, first-time buyers. Back then, my step-father owned a construction company. He remodelled homes and sometimes built a few too, as opportunities arose for him to purchase vacant lots. The real estate market was slow, and he was having difficulty selling one home he had built in a town about 40 minutes from where we lived. Chris and I were already planning to get married that summer, and had started looking around town at the rental market. When my mom and step-father mentioned the idea of having us purchase the home, we jumped at the idea. Especially since they would somehow work out the deal for us to have no down payment. With only a couple thousand our bank accounts, this was the only way it could possibly work! Zero down (or even 3% down) was not commonplace like it is now. Home loans were harder to get, and paying 10-20% down was typically required back then.

After some searching, and with our very little credit history, we eventually found a company willing to loan to us. Although they thoroughly raked us over the coals with an 11% interest rate, by golly we had our own house. It felt good, but looking back, I don't know if I'd do it again.

We lived there for about 2.5 years before deciding to sell the home. The neighborhood and setting was peaceful and nice, with treed lots and simple homes, but it was a 40-minute drive to work for both of us Monday-Friday. The long commute got old, hardly anyone came to visit and our gas bill was massive. Since housing prices had barely appreciated at all, we walked away from that sale with only $1500. Not a great return on investment. I suppose if we'd rented all that time, we would have walked away with not a cent. However, expenses in the meantime would have been cheaper. Renting at that time may have been wiser.

We lived paycheck to paycheck in that little house. We'd take long walks in the evenings when the weather was nice, discussing the many dreams and goals we had for our future. Unfortunately, while we dreamed, we also racked up credit card debt and owned expensive cars we never should have had.

Being a young couple with no money left at the end of the month and a big house payment (for us it was big then), we were "stuff poor." The stuff we had held us back financially. All our hard-earned money went towards paying for stuff, most of it which we could have done without (or at least we should have had a less-expensive version of it).

> Stuff poor: when a person or family's stuff (cars, homes, furniture, electronics, tools, toys, boats, etc.) causes financial lack, even when the stuff's payments can be "afforded."

Looking back at those early decisions, if I had it to do over again, here's what I'd do differently:

- Rent an inexpensive home near our workplaces
- Had dependable, nice, older cars without loans
- Save money, therefore being able to pay cash for things

we really needed rather than using credit cards
- Not spend money on lame MLM or get-rich-quick ideas

Yes, we did that too a few times. Not all MLM or network marketing companies are lame schemes, by the way, but the one we got involved in back then was. I had the bug even back then for wanting to create financial increase. We bought a couple vending machines. We signed up for a travel MLM company. We bought info products from (supposed) financial gurus. I tried side business ideas like a serial killer – always looking for the next target. We were going about it in all the wrong ways, shooting without aiming, not even sure what to aim for. It was a disaster. None of it created increase. All these efforts subtracted from our finances.

After selling our house, we lived with my dad in his basement for a year. Not completely free of bad spending habits yet, but things were improving. We paid my dad a certain amount each month, which helped us and him. We were able to save some money up, knowing we wanted to buy another home in town in the near future. When a house one mile away came up for sale by owner, we made an offer and bought the home. It was in serious need of updating (everything was original from the 70's), but had great bones and the location was great. Room by room we made updates to flooring, countertops, paint, tile and more during the seven years we lived there.

Within the first year of buying that house, we made another financial decision I would never do again: we bought a brand new—pick your colors out, delivered on a car carrier truck—car. At the time, we still had our credit card debt as well, plus purchased some new furniture on a six-months same-as-cash deal. Thank God we had the sense to pay that furniture off before the six months was up, but all our debt and payments started becoming annoying. We weren't getting ahead, although we looked like we were doing just fine. We were, I suppose. Every month we faithfully paid our bills and payments, but something still felt wrong.

Back then, we thought we were affording all of these things without any issues. Could we afford the payment? "Okay then, no worries!" was our mantra. But, we did not understand this concept at all yet:

If you can't pay cash, you can't really afford it.

You may be thinking of your home loan after reading that. Everyone must have a place to live, and very few can pay cash for their home, so we view home debt somewhat differently. Although renting does make more financial sense in some cases. But I digress…we'll talk more about real estate in a different chapter.

By this time, we were attending church together, learning more about living life according to God's ways. The little church we went to didn't have financial teaching and we weren't able to give much. But, something was shifting in our hearts, slowly but surely. We wanted to be more generous. It's hard to be generous when you're stuff poor. It's hard to get ahead at all financially when you're stuff poor.

If money could talk, I imagine it would say something like this:

Spend (consume) some of me and
grow (invest) the rest of me.

For each one of us, many influences have shaped our spending habits – parents, friends, marketing, advertisements and media sources, our community/location where we live, social media, co-workers, neighbors, and more. Some of these influence us at a subconscious level (the general world around us), some shape us through role modeling and what's become our normal (close relationships and family), and others have a strategic, intentional plan to reach into our wallets (marketing and advertisements).

The two biggest influencers of how we spend money are our closest relationships and the media messages we constantly see. Our emotions have even become involved. Sometimes even our identity has become wrapped up in our spending habits. *Why* we buy stuff can be more complex than we think!

Am I buying lots of makeup, beauty and hair treatments, nails, tanning, or even plastic surgery because I feel the need to impress people, I'm seeking their approval, I'm lonely and need to feel valuable, peer pressure, or I have to keep up my ultra-fancy image? That's just one simple example of how emotions and identity are at work in our finances.

Much bigger examples of it occur every day across America. Compelled to keep up an image, many sabotage their financial futures.

Overspending

You've probably heard the question before: "Are you a spender or a saver?" If you're very young, you may not have figured this out yet, but as you start out your financial life, it becomes fairly clear, quickly. For you spenders, overkill can come in the form of overspending if you're not careful. The problem is evident when debt racks up; debt for stuff beyond basic needs.

The habit of overspending may derive from the modeling we had when growing up – either we had nothing and now want to overly make up for it by buying too much, or we were modeled the habit of overspending. It could also be caused by emotions, like greed, low self-esteem or fear. *Having all this will make people like me.* Go big or go home. Excess, excess, excess.

Underspending

For you savers, overkill can also come to you in the form of underspending. This is a term you may not be familiar with yet. Our money persona, Miser Matt, has this problem. Miser Matt is so focused on scarcity that he doesn't spend a penny even if he really should. Even for safety or basic needs, underspenders want to put a lock on their wallets. They somehow think they're getting ahead, but it may cause other areas of their lives (relationships, health, well-being) to fall behind.

As an example, the generation of people who grew up in the Great Depression era had their minds seared by lack. It's what they saw and experienced, and like a relentless shadow, lack was with them every day. These types of experiences have a way of shaping a person's outlook, understandably. But, there is a line between being frugal and underspending. Underspenders look for ways to keep their lives small and controlled, no matter if their financial situation has greatly improved and lack isn't actually there anymore (other than in their minds).

We'll talk more about the pitfalls of underspending later.

Compulsive Spending

Let's be honest, this type of spending isn't helpful for our health, our waistbands or our wallets. Be careful anytime you hear yourself saying, "I *need* my _____," (fill in the blank).

I need my…
Coffee	Energy drink
Wine	Mani/pedi
Beer	Casino
Shopping therapy	New shoes
Chocolate	Latest tech item or game
Cookies/donuts	

None of those things are truly a need. You can be perfectly happy without them completely! Although in moderation (and without desperation) and self-control, spending wisely on these things from time to time is just fine.

The problem comes when these wants become must haves. There's a compulsion or pull, and then you know there's a problem, and it's sure to hit your wallet in some way. "Without this, you won't be happy," the advertisers say, and then you may start to tell it to yourself, too.

Spending on Destructive Habits

Chances are we won't die from spending a lot on coffee or manicures. However, spending on certain types of items can cause people serious physical, emotional, relational, and/or mental harm. A few examples are:

Smoking
Alcoholism
Drug Abuse
Gambling
Sex Industry, Porn and Adult Entertainment

Any addictions are harmful to your overall quality of life – food, substance, sex, etc. Let's talk about the sex industry for a moment as an example.

Wait a minute, you may be thinking, *isn't this book supposed to be about money?* Yes, yes it is. Here's why this discussion is important. The *so-called* adult entertainment sex industry is not your friend. Strangely, their goal is to *enslave your imagination* in order to get to your wallet. Your money is their ultimate target. They don't care about you, your needs, your soul or your heart...at all. Strip clubs...all about money. Porn magazines and websites...want your money and the advertisers' money. And even more dangerous and dark is human trafficking. That's all about money as well. If no one ever paid for porn, prostitution or "adult entertainment," it would all go away today.

Having involvement with any of these destructive habits usually leads to mental, physical, emotional or spiritual problems such as relationship breakdowns, health crises and disease, sexual dysfunction, depression, anxiety, mental illness, low self-worth, suicidal thoughts, anger, legal and criminal problems, work and career breakdown, and financial collapse. Or, these destructive habits amplify and worsen these conditions if they were already there.

If you're struggling with any of these destructive habits and find yourself suffering with any of these mental, physical, emotional or spiritual problems, seek help today. You may feel trapped and powerless. Addiction is real. It wants to steal your personal power, your will and future (and money). But, every decision is ultimately in your hands. You don't have to live like this anymore. Your life is too valuable to waste one more day on addiction. We urge you to find freedom, and if you need any help finding real help, please let us know. Millions of others have fought addiction and won the battle, and now are living with hope and freedom.

Why Am I Spending?

For the sake of our spending habits discussion, glossing over the fact that spending issues can stem from internal pain, unmet emotional needs or sadness in our souls would do you a disservice. These are real struggles many people are experiencing right now. As you spend, ask yourself a lot of questions to see what's going on inside you.

Why am I buying this?
Do I think this is going to somehow increase my happiness?
Is this purchase wrapped up in an identity or emotional issue?
Do I feel a compulsion to buy this? Why?
Do I truly want this item?
Do I think others will like me better if I own this?
Is this item good for me?
Does buying or owning this somehow stoke my ego or pride?
Does this purchase move me closer to my financial goals or further away?

Will I regret this purchase tomorrow, next week, next year, etc.?

These questions will help you get in touch with your inner motivations/motives. Nearly all of our actions and decisions stem from there. Be on the lookout especially for the urge to spend that's motivated by any self-worth issues, greed, prideful identity or compulsions. By asking yourself tough questions, it may just change your life!

Let's use a simple example of a product people spend on that may be connected to mindset or emotions: fake nails. There's nothing wrong with fake nails at all, but I'm going to use them as an example of something to evaluate; something that's unnecessary, but often purchased by people. If you're a guy, of course fake nails don't apply to you, but hopefully you'll get the point. Think about:

Why are fake nails a priority to me?
Could I buy a multivitamin and improve my overall health (and nails in the process) instead?
Could I do without them for a while in order to save money for a greater purpose?
Do I think people will like me better if I have cute, fake nails?
Will I like me better if I have cute, fake nails? Why?
Or, will I like me better if I have a handle on my finances and a bunch of money in the bank?

My point is to get us to ask ourselves why doing, buying or "needing" certain things feels like a priority, even when spending money on it is unnecessary and could take away from our bigger financial goals. I'm not advocating that we deprive ourselves of every treat or fun frill in life, but to consider our actions, habits, belief systems and our future. My point is…just think about it a bit more.

If you have no debt, a good income, money in the bank, all the physical needs covered for your family, you're being generous, and you want to get some fake nails…well then you go girl! The $50 you may be spending per month isn't going to bother your budget much. However, if you're struggling to pay rent, keep gas in your car, buy your kids a pair of shoes or pay a bill, spending $50 on nails is absolutely nonsensical. I know people who do this.

If you're in a tough spot like this and you're regularly spending hundreds on cigarettes, fast food, fancy daily coffee drinks, beer, wine, or memberships you don't use (just to name a few), you might as well take a blowtorch to your wallet. But, please don't torch your finances through needless spending – it's just not wise. Maybe no one has ever been straightforward enough to tell you that before.

Just Plain Bad Habits

Beyond the emotional side of our spending, sometimes we've just learned some bad habits! Here are a few we've heard of or (sadly) have even done ourselves:

- Taking money out of a HELOC (home equity line of credit) or getting a loan to take family vacations
- Buying brand new cars, just because
- Buying fixer cars (or boats, or…) that you never actually fix, and they become permanent yard fixtures!

- Buying lots of "big-boy toys" that rarely get used
- Not researching before making a large purchase (impulse buying)
- Shopping at the mall as a hobby
- Hoarding

And, here are two other bad habits you may have learned:

- Not making generosity a priority
- Not spending (wisely) on items or services that improve your health and safety

Some people are so frugal, they won't even spend on vitamins, necessary medications, fixing safety or health issues in their homes or cars, dentist visits, clean water, adequate heat, healthy food, etc. Have you ever seen someone do this? We have, and it most likely stems from fear of some kind. A scarcity mindset may cause them to hold tightly to every penny, even if their health or safety is at risk. It's one thing to absolutely not have the money for it right now, but it's quite another to have the money and not be willing to spend it.

Regarding generosity, some people have never experienced their family or friends being financially generous towards causes and organizations that make a meaningful difference in the lives of people. Opportunities exist everywhere to put generosity into practice. Help a struggling family directly, give to organizations that do important work in your community, tithe to a church, sponsor a kid to go to summer camp, do random acts of kindness and gift-giving, fix a single parent's car, support a charitable organization or orphanage, and endless more ideas. Again, a scarcity mindset could be keeping a person from generosity. *If I give, there won't be enough for me…*

But there's good news! If we recognize our bad habits, we can take steps to change and replace them. Sometimes it can feel embarrassing to recognize our own shortcomings, but seeing and acknowledging them gives us an amazing opportunity to be better.

Setting Your Spending Priorities

Take a look at this infographic. We call it the Spending Priority Pyramid. The Spending Priority Pyramid is based on purpose, vision, goals and needs/wants. The most important items are at the top, flowing down in priority from there.

Needed to Live
Necessary Spending
Special Savings Priorities
Not connected to purpose or happiness spending
Not important or worthless spending

Each individual or couple should take a bit of time to determine what belongs on each level. What are the priorities for your household?

The *I-need-this-to-live* tier would be pretty much the same for all of us: food/water, housing and clothes. As far as spending goes, those are a person's most basic needs. But, a lot can vary within those three items from person to person! Housing looks a lot different for different people though, right? Anything from a tent to a mansion. We'll talk more about that later.

Necessary Spending might be similar for many of us. At our house, necessary spending is typically our monthly bills such as cell phones, insurance, medical, birthday and holiday gifts, Internet service, car and home maintenance, education costs, and utilities. Most of them aren't glamourous, but our household won't run quite right without these. Not everyone, though, will consider all of these *necessary*.

Beyond those things, Chris and I have these two items in our Special Savings Priorities: travel and investing. If we're saving money, those are the things we're saving for.

Although we've tried to minimize spending in the bottom two tiers, it's inevitable that dorky stuff slips in from time to time! School fundraisers, that pair of running shoes (despite not running anymore), pedicures, eating out…again, the as-seen-on-TV gadget, the fancy chrome grill and a muffler kit for a used car, coffee shops, magazines, those pretty earrings, that pretty motorcycle…you get the idea. *None* of these things are truly necessary.

If you give it an honest look and discover you are spending more than is wise in the bottom tier (Not Important or Worthless Spending), our suggestion is to immediately stop spending one more dollar on those things, especially if you're in a dire financial situation. It's a waste. And, if you need a drastic change for your spending habits, take a very close look at both the bottom two tiers. You may need to go on a money diet for a certain period of time, and those two tiers are ideal to cut out of your *consumption*.

Your tiers may look very different or maybe somewhat similar. Take a moment to write out what fills up your tiers. Are there changes you could make?

Your Special Savings Priorities is Key

It may take you a few minutes to determine your Special Savings Priorities tier. However, defining what's in this one is crucial. That's where your goals and plans live. What's in this tier anchors you to something better for the future.

When Chris and I decide *not* to make a purchase or spend frivolously on unnecessary things, what's on this tier is why. These two (and maybe you'll have just one or maybe three…) are so important to us, so central in our financial goals, that they influence most of our spending (and saving) decisions.

It's possible that paying off debt is on your Special Savings Priorities tier. For several years, paying off debt was all that was in that tier for us. Student loans, car loans, consumer credit card debt, personal loans, taxes, and other money you owe feels heavy. It weighs on a person's emotions, relationships and sometimes on a person's ability to dream about their future. It limits opportunities. I believe that's why this saying exists: "Getting *out from under* debt." The weight, pressure or burden of debt can be anywhere from annoying to unbearable. The heavier the load, the more unbearable it becomes.

If that's your situation right now, make every effort to pay off your debts as soon as humanly possible. You'll be thrilled when that day comes. Imagine what that will feel like! You can go from where you are now to a place of blissful freedom. How? By a combination of things:

- Change your money mindsets and spending habits
- Set a budget
- Bring more money into your monthly budget

That's it! And that's why we do what we do at The Abundance Plan. If you put *pay off debt* in your Special Savings Priorities tier, you'll shift your focus, anchoring your spending decisions to your plans for being debt free. Having a clear picture of and a focus on the happiness of being debt free and escaping the debt-burden pain you're experiencing now is an effective motivator.

> *"Wealth consists not in having great possessions, but in having few wants."* –Epictetus

Needed to Live
Necessary Spending
Special Savings Priorities
Not connected to purpose or happiness spending
Not important or worthless spending

Note: Special savings priorities will change over time, depending on what phase of life you're in. See our *The Abundance Plan Workbook* for a fill-in-the-blank Spending Priority Pyramid, plus many other helpful worksheets.

Change is Required

A few years ago, a couple we knew asked Chris and I if we could help them figure out their finances. They had many debts, although were both working and had fairly good incomes. As we talked, they voiced their desire to get out of debt. As we talked more, it became clear they were not willing to endure the pain of a crunch-time season in order to obtain the promise of a debt-free life. It became clear that their true priority was pleasure and not being debt-free.

One of the comments was, "You mean we can't go on our vacations?" My inside voice thought this: *Umm, well, it's up to you, but not if you want to get out of debt anytime soon. And, it's not like that will be the case forever, but it sounds like you'll be choosing to stay in the exact same financial position for quite some time…*

> *"Many love the idea of change and freedom, but they're really not committed to it."* –Pedro Adao

Had they decided to save up in advance for vacations and travel, then awesome! Great plan! But, no…every whim was put on a credit card. That's exactly like a person saying they want to lose 15 lbs, but they keep eating large bowls of ice cream every day. They really don't want to lose weight. They really want to keep eating ice cream. They're wishing for the weight to leave, magically, with no effort.

It all comes down to choices. Make choices that support what you say you want, and what you say you want probably comes from the deepest, truest part of you.

Sometimes the truth hurts. But, to each his own, as they say. If a person truly wants a change, then there has to be a... change.

Change is simple, but change is not always easy. A good question to ask ourselves is:

>**"Am I willing to endure change,
>even if only for a season?"**

Chapter 3

Self-Control

Now that you've read the spending habits chapter, it's time to tackle the next topic: self-control. Sorry if your teeth grit and knuckles whiten at the mere mention of it! But consider this powerful truth: if a person can improve their self-control skills, it will have a positive effect on every area of their life. Every. Single. Area. Forever.

Self-control is the follow-up action for your goals and plans.

You say you want to go to the next level with your finances, now what are you going to do about it?

It's where the rubber meets the road, as they say. With every goal you have, self-control will help you attain it.

"The biggest gap in your life is that between what you know and what you do." –Bob Proctor

For a road trip, you need a vehicle and a map, right? Imagine that your life is the vehicle, the map is your plan, the destination is your goal, and self-control is how the vehicle is steered (the steering wheel). Without a destination (goal) in mind, you'll wander aimlessly. Without the map (a clear plan), you'll get lost and frustrated. And without a steering wheel (self-control), you won't get anywhere you hope to go. The ditch will be calling. Self-control will steer you towards your desired destinations and away from pitfalls and dangers.

Discipline

Discipline can seem like a scary word, but it has several definitions:

1. Punishment and correction for wrong, illegal or undesirable actions.
2. A field of study or knowledge.
3. Training oneself to have consistent, established habits or courses of action, leading to better results.

Number three applies to finances, because it's all about self-control. And, a person lacking it may also experience discipline definition number one! Yikes...

The temporary pain of learning to be disciplined and practicing self-control will always be miniscule in comparison to the pain of regret.

Discipline and self-control are partially about telling yourself *no*. No, I choose not to buy this right now. No, I'm saving money for an important investment. No, I won't use my credit card for that.

They're also partially about saying *yes*. Yes, I tell my money where to go and not the other way around. Yes, having a budget makes a big difference for me. Yes, I'm getting better with financial stewardship. Yes, I have other goals. Yes, I can do this. Say yes to your dreams, no to distractions and temptations.

Back to definition number three: training oneself to have consistent, established habits or courses of action, leading to better results. A person can have self-control once or twice, but discipline is the consistency. I can say *no* to the donut on Tuesday, which was great self-control for that moment. But when Wednesday rolls around, I eat five. My habit and course of action was not consistent. Discipline was lacking.

If my current habit is to eat donuts every day, then my donut-free Tuesday was a small victory and should be celebrated (but not with a cookie…). Every step in the right direction is a good thing. Discipline is the part where you retrain yourself to have new habits and actions. Habits become automatic actions we routinely take. Some of our current habits help us (like brushing our teeth everyday) and some do not (like biting fingernails). The best advice is to make a good decision, and then automate it somehow.

> *"When it comes to budgeting, saving money and building wealth, successful people realize that if left to a conscious decision at the end of each month, it will probably never happen…They realize that by using systems to automate their financial habits, they can make steady progress towards their goals over time."* –Curtis Hearn, CFP, Investopedia

The military comes up when I think of discipline. A drill sergeant's duty is to whip their soldiers into shape—physical and mental shape—training them to think and act differently than they're used to. Although their methods may be harsh at times, they are effective.

Keep Your Eye on the Prize

Retraining yourself to think and act differently about your money doesn't need to be severe or feel like punishment. In fact, it could be like a game.

As a kid, did you ever go to a birthday party with a piñata? You know, the colorful paper mache shapes that hang from a string, filled with goodies? Oh, the glory of it…the anticipation…the build up…and them the BOOM! The prize bursts out, spilling everywhere for everyone to enjoy.

What if you had a "Debt Piñata" that you stuffed with goodies, notes or special things, and you took a bat to it when your debt gets paid off? How fun! That's my silly idea, and here are a few others from some of my friends:

- Find friends to celebrate with you along the way as you hit milestones.
- Chart your progress.
- Reward yourself with a campout, hike or drive to the beach or lake.
- Make it a game to see how much you can save or pay down debt per month and use a chart.
- Create a challenge group with friends or family for encouragement, accountability and celebration.
- Make a dream or vision board.
- Set aside a small amount of "fun money" after reaching certain milestones along the way.

In any case, being more disciplined and having self-control doesn't have to be drudgery. It's actually a really cool thing!

> *"We need to make a game out of earning money. There is so much good we can do with money. Without it, we are bound and shackled and our choices become limited."* –Bob Proctor

Delayed Gratification

I once heard an interesting study done with elementary-school-aged children. They took a group of kids and placed a donut in front of each child and gave them two options:

Option 1: You can eat this donut right now.
Option 2: If you don't eat this donut now, you can have three donuts tomorrow.

From what I remember, a larger percentage of the kiddos gobbled up the donut sitting right in front of their face rather than waiting for their promised larger prize tomorrow. Now, believe me, I am definitely a fan of donuts. For me, not eating the one sitting there right then would've been difficult. But also, since I love donuts, not waiting for three tomorrow would have given me more thoughts to chew on (pun intended). One mindset says *right now is better, even if it's less*. The other says *more is better, even if it's tomorrow*.

Psychologists believed this small test or demonstration was telling; indicating how good or not-so-good these kids would be when it comes to delayed gratification as they grew up. What would you do?

Wait For It...

As the decades march on, it seems like our culture and society has an ever increasingly difficult time with the concept of waiting. Instant gratification seems to be preferred. I'm guilty of the waiting frustration myself in some ways: waiting in lines, waiting in traffic, waiting for someone to make a decision, etc. But, financially, I understand that waiting often has benefits and includes a multiplication factor.

> *"Patience is a virtue and the best things in life are worth waiting for."* –Julie Spira

Anything highly valuable and secure in life takes some time to build. Trust is earned. Education is a process. Relationships form over time. Money's multiplication factor takes time.

Money is like a seed. When you eat all your seeds, there's nothing left to plant (save and invest). When you can't plant, you can't grow more. If we're able to restrain our craving for instant gratification, we're on our way to wisdom, and wisdom creates abundance.

Self-Control Summary

- With every goal a person has, self-control helps them achieve it.
- Self-control will steer you towards your desired destinations and away from pitfalls and dangers.
- Getting your finances on track can be fun! Be creative about celebrating your milestones.
- Habits become automatic actions we routinely take.
- Delayed gratification can seem annoying at the time, but it can lead to bigger, lasting blessing.

Chapter 4

Bye-Bye Debt

"Among the 73 percent of consumers who had debt when they died, about 68 percent had credit card balances. The next most common kind of debt was mortgage debt (37 percent), followed by auto loans (25 percent), personal loans (12 percent) and student loans (6 percent)."
–Christine DiGangi, Credit.com

For anyone who has ever been in debt, you can testify of its displeasure: from nuisance to anguish. Because debt is stressful and heavy, it can even diminish a person's ability to be creative and dream about their future. Remorse and regret are ingredients in debt's recipe. Of course, not all debt comes from poor or impulsive decisions. Life happens sometimes, despite our best efforts and good habits.

"A man in debt is so far a slave."
–Ralph Waldo Emerson

Unexpected medical emergencies and expenses are a clear example of *life-happens* debt. Most of the time, however, the vast majority of debt issues come from our habits and choices. This is good news though, because we have the power to change our habits and choices, creating a better future for ourselves.

"Do something today your tomorrow self will thank you for."
–Krista Dunk

Consumer Debt

Respect yourself: the today you *and* the tomorrow you. One of the best financial ways to respect yourself is to avoid going into consumer debt. Taking on debt for vehicles, furniture, clothing, electronics, RV's, ATV's, vacations, entertainment, appliances, beauty services, eating out, and other stuff can be a trap.

As of 2018, Americans are paying over $100 billion in credit card interest and fees every year, and numbers estimated for 2019 will be closer to $110 billion (according to FDIC data analyzed by Magnify Money/LendingTree). Those numbers are so big, I have a hard time comprehending them.

Credit card companies and banks are enticing and binding consumers with debt because of greed, but it works both ways. Financial companies are greedy for the interest and fees they earn, and consumers are greedy for bigger, better and more stuff. Of our own will we're being enslaved. It's sad, but true.

You don't have to participate in this cycle of greed! If you're one of the fortunate ones who doesn't have consumer debt right now, keep up the good work. Continue to avoid debt as much as possible. If you have debt now, we'll talk about that next. Taking on debt for real estate, business or education can be viewed a bit differently. We'll talk more about that later.

In a recent *Rich Dad, Poor Dad Daily* newsletter, Robert Kiyosaki wrote about five things he and his wife did to rid themselves of debt after they got married. I'm going to paraphrase these five helpful steps.

1. Stop accruing consumer debt immediately. Adding to your credit card balances doesn't help you.
2. Make a comprehensive list of all your current debts (all loans, IOU's, credit cards, etc.).
3. Hire a bookkeeper, CPA or coach to keep you accountable and so your info is kept current.
4. Still set a percentage aside to "pay yourself" first. Use this money to save, for charitable giving and investing.
5. Employ a Debt Snowball method for paying off each debt you currently owe.

If you are in debt now, chances are you're reading this because you need a change. You want something different and need a plan. Getting out of debt might be the next big step along your financial path. The most effective plan we've used to eliminate debt is the Debt Snowball.

Debt Snowball

In his *Financial Peace University* books and classes, Dave Ramsey likes to teach about the "Debt Snowball," as he calls it. The concept is quite simple: focus on paying off one debt at a time, and then roll the money you had paid on the first one onto the next debt, paying it off, and the process continues (assuming you have three, four, five, etc., to pay off). For people who want to become debt free, it's a great plan. We recommend reading *Financial Peace University* for the Debt Snowball and budgeting sections. Also see *The Abundance Plan Workbook* for a handy debt payoff chart.

Example:
You have three debts: a car loan, a boat loan and a credit card balance. You owe $15,000 on your car, $11,500 on your boat

and $12,000 on your credit card. Figure out which one has the worst interest rate (most likely the credit card) and direct any and all extra money you can come up with to pay down that balance each month. Let's target paying off the credit card. By the way, some people choose to target the debt that has the lowest balance owed first. But whether it's the debt with the largest interest rate or lowest balance, pick one to payoff first.

Let's say your minimum monthly payment on this credit card balance is $200, and you scraped, scrimped and made a plan to come up with $300 more (totaling $500). Pay $500 to the credit card bill and continue to pay only the minimum monthly payments on the car and boat loans. This is key – be sure to keep paying all the other minimum monthly payments or missing those payments will destroy your credit score!

Once your credit card is paid off (for God's sake don't rack up any more on it), use all the $500 money you were sending to the credit card bill each month, plus the minimum you paid on your boat loan (let's say $300), and plop it all ($800) on the boat loan next to pay it off (assuming the boat had the next worst interest rate). Pay off and repeat. With a big $800 chunk hitting that boat loan balance every month, you'll be surprised at how quickly it will be paid off.

> *"There is scarcely anything that drags a person down like debt."* –P. T. Barnum

Once all your debts are paid off, you'll suddenly find yourself with a large chunk of money each month freed up! Imagine that! This is when the financial magic can start to happen. Once you've gone through this process, you will have a huge sense of accomplishment and will most likely never be tempted to rack up debt like that ever again.

I believe the Debt Snowball process works very well when paying down debt. If you got really serious, you could even keep going and take the extra money and roll it into paying down your home mortgage (or save up for a home down payment). Chris and I are doing exactly that right now.

About eight years ago, our church had a small group teaching series about getting out of debt and whipping your finances into shape. Chris and I were group leaders, and we assumed there wouldn't be much for us to get out of the series. *This may not help us much,* we thought. The only debt we had at the time was our home loan. But, we were wrong.

After about week three, a light bulb came on. We finished the group having a plan in place to pay our mortgage off within five years (shaving off nearly 15 years of our 20-year loan…yes you read that right). There was something valuable in that group study for us after all.

After paying bills and our house payment, we had been shifting all the extra money into our savings account…for a rainy day I guess. Instead, we used extra money from paychecks to pay down the house loan. We already had a good buffer in our savings account, and putting more in there wasn't doing any good. The 1% interest we were earning on it was pitiful. Sending that extra money to pay off the house that had a 4.5% interest rate loan was smarter.

In the meantime, we sold that home and have purchased a new one, and have implemented the same strategy. In case you're wondering how we do this, since we have no other debts, we double our house payment each month. It's shocking how fast this slashes away at the balance. Even paying one extra payment per year has a big impact on a home loan's balance. Some people like to divide one payment up by 12 and add the extra on monthly, and some prefer to pay one extra payment all at once.

To Pay Off, or Not to Pay Off

When it comes to paying off your home mortgage, a few more considerations come into play. However, I do not buy the mantra from traditional financial planners who say *never* pay it off early. I'm skeptical about why they're advising that. They cite the tax write-off benefit for mortgage interest paid each year, but what is their true motivation for advising people to keep home loan debt? Do they benefit somehow from people keeping that debt? Do they work for a bank or mortgage company who's raking in the interest? Possibly there are other factors involved.

I think because we always heard the *keep-your-home-loan* "advice" from professionals so often was why Chris and I had never really considered paying off our home loan early before. But after our church's small group series on finances, we imagined the bliss of being mortgage free.

> *"Jesus made it plain when He said, "You cannot serve both God and money." Yet many people serve money without ever making a conscious choice to do so. By not learning how to manage our money, we become servants to our finances."*
> –Billy Epperhardt, author of *Money Mastery*

There are others who advise paying off your home as fast as you can. Their arguments make more sense to me. If you have a $1400 monthly payment for example, not including any property taxes or insurance, approximately $1000 of that goes to interest for the first six years. Six years of $1000 vanishing into thin air every month is a tough pill to swallow. As you near the end of your loan term, 24 years later, it won't be as bad. By then your interest amount per month will be very low, around $200 or less of your payment amount. The lower the balance owed, the interest portion of your monthly payment becomes less. But how many people live in the same home for 30 years anymore? A few do, but not many.

As you can see in the chart I inserted next, if you have a $290,000 original mortgage amount at 4.5% interest rate for 30 years, you'll end up paying $528,979 for your home loan (total principal paid plus total interest paid). That's a LOT of wasted money; *your* money. Interest is not your friend unless you're earning it.

Mortgage amount	Monthly Payments
$ 290,000	$1,469.39
Mortgage term in years	
30	Total Principal Paid — $290,000
Or	Total Interest Paid — $238,979.46
Term in months	
360	
Interest rate per year	TODAY'S RATES
4.5 % CALCULATE	Hide amortization schedule

If you visit www.bankrate.com/calculators/mortgages, you can calculate home loan payments, see interest amounts by viewing amortization schedules, see how making extra payments would affect your loan, plus get other helpful information.

The faster you pay down the principle balance of your loan, the faster you get to the point of paying less interest every month. Sure, you may have $12,000 in mortgage interest to write off on your taxes. But how much of a tax break will that really give you? It depends on your tax bracket, and it reduces your taxable income when taken as an itemized deduction. It could reduce your tax bill by $3000-$4000. Still not worth it in my opinion. Spending $12,000 to get $3500 is crazy. It doesn't make financial sense at all, and those in the financial world who advise it are doing us a disservice. I'd rather owe the IRS $3500 each April. I'd save myself $8500.

Certainly, pay off your house mortgage UNLESS using up all your available cash to do so prevents you from having a safety net and growing your money. For example, if you take your savings down to $2000 in order to pay your house loan off early, that's probably not ideal. It's too risky. Having some cash on hand for emergencies and unexpected expenses is imperative. Also, some people prefer to have a certain amount of cash on hand in case investment opportunities come along.

Here's another consideration. If your house loan's interest rate is low (somewhere around 4%), could you put your money to work for you in an investment earning a higher rate of return than 4%, rather than spending that money on paying the loan off early? This is where starting to think differently about money will help you make better decisions.

Here's an example of what I mean: if you were thinking about adding $750 every month ($9,000 per year) to your mortgage payment in order to pay the loan off faster, is there an investment opportunity where that $9,000 could safely earn 6%, 7%, 8% or more? If so, it logically makes more sense to put it in the investment. Although emotionally it may feel better to have your house paid off. That's a decision only you can make for yourself.

If you have a terrible interest rate on your mortgage, then that's also something to consider in this decision. You could think about refinancing your high interest rate loan to get a better interest rate if you plan to stay in that same home for at least four more years. Don't bother refinancing if you plan to sell soon. Loan officers have told me the numbers don't make sense to refinance if you'll be moving soon when you factor in the cost of the fees. But in recent years, home mortgage interest rates have been between 3%-5%, which is excellent. If you do refinance, and you can still afford the same monthly payment amount you've been paying, consider refinancing to a 20-year or 15-year mortgage term with a lower rate. It shaves time, and therefore interest, off your loan. And don't be tempted to get cash out of your refinance unless you desperately, *desperately* need to do so.

Rental Property Mortgages

Note, if you own rental properties with loans, some suggest allowing other people's money (OPM) to pay off the loans without worrying about paying them off early. I see why they suggest it, because incoming rent money typically covers the payment plus giving the owner (hopefully) a bit of monthly cash flow. Sometimes a landlord may need the cash flow to supplement their income. Maybe they aren't able to dedicate more money towards paying that loan off early. In other cases landlords bank the cash flow, save it up and use it to purchase their next property, assuming they don't need the cash flow to supplement their own monthly income. In either of these instances, I see the logic in not taking extra cash to pay off their rental's loan early.

However, again, paying less interest on a loan equals more money eventually in your pocket...always. If a landlord has several rentals, and doesn't need the cash flow for their own living expenses and doesn't plan to buy additional properties anytime soon, why not target one of the loans with a pay-down plan, sort of like a Debt Snowball? For example:

Rental #1 - $1300 payment. $1550 rent collected. Cash flow = $250
Rental #2 - $1050 payment. $1500 rent collected. Cash flow = $450
Rental #3 - $1100 payment. $1500 rent collected. Cash flow = $400
Total monthly payments = $3450. Total monthly cash flow = $1100.

Which loan has the highest interest rate? Or which property has the lowest remaining loan balance? Let's say property #3 does. Do a Debt Snowball and pay the minimum payments on properties #1 and #2, and take the $1100 cash flow and use it all on #3 (making a monthly payment of $2200). Once that loan is paid off, use the cash flow to target one of the remaining loans next. It would be wise to have at least four months of the cash flow saved up before doing this though. Expenses, repairs and vacancies do happen.

This strategy would be most appropriate for a landlord who knows they'll need more cash flow in the near future (and don't need it now). If they plan to retire in ten years from their regular job, this could work very well. When all of these properties are paid off, all that's left are property taxes and insurance (and some occasional repairs). The rest is cash flow (of about $3000) in the landlord's hand every month, and that doesn't even account for increasing rent prices that are bound to happen as time goes on. Even if there's a vacancy at that point, no biggie if there's no mortgage due.

In any case, take a serious look at paying down and paying off mortgages faster than the loan term and see if it makes good financial sense. It would be worth having a conversation with your CPA or tax preparer. There are a lot of factors to consider.

Income Snowball?

As you can see, the idea of a Debt Snowball is exciting. But what about this: what if there was an *Income Snowball*? That's an even more exciting thought. I just made it up! As we plan and set goals for our financial future, I believe there are ways to grow wealth and make our money work for us beyond savings accounts and 401Ks. Money can actually be used to make more money, without us working more.

"When it comes to budgeting, you can only get your spending down to zero. But, there's no limit to your amount of income. Increase your income and manage expenses." –Jim Baker

Our educational system is very focused on teaching us how to be good employees. Even typical financial advisors cater their solutions and advice to the working class. This is not necessarily bad, other than we're just not getting the whole story. Very, very few people become wealthy by having a job and being an employee. Sure, you can save and save and do pretty well as a well-paid, higher income-earning employee, but people who truly find financial freedom almost always obtain it through other means of income. They have some kind of Income Snowball.

Think about everyone you know who's exceptionally wealthy. Not those who have the appearance of wealth and are in monthly payments up to their eyeballs...but those who are really abundant. A true, independently wealthy person can enjoy their money, be generous and have more than enough without having to think about scrimping constantly.

I don't know about you, but I've had very few examples of people with this type of financial freedom in my life. Nearly everyone I know who is doing "well" with money and finances has had an employee mindset, combined with good spending and saving habits. The people I know who are well-off employees live conservative lives, save money, don't have outlandish spending habits, and know how to do everything a regular financial advisor would recommend. It's what we've been taught. It's what we're used to. But, is our "normal" the highest and best way?

Debt Summary

- Debt can feel like an emotional weight and can dim the ability to dream and be creative.

- Make a plan to pay off consumer debt and loans as soon as possible, even including your home loan.
- Dave Ramsey's Debt Snowball method is an excellent, accelerated way to pay debts off one-by-one.

Chapter 5

Setting Goals for Your Financial Future

"I love it when a plan comes together."
–John "Hannibal" Smith, *The A-Team*

I read a story a few years ago about a single man who had a big goal: pay off his new home's loan in five years or less. It didn't sound like he was a high-income earner, which made his big goal seem a bit outlandish. But as soon as he bought his house, he put his plan into action. He had a whatever-it-takes approach, which included things like eating ramen and other cheap food, not going to movies or paying for any entertainment (only free), not paying for travel (only doing free activities), no cable, riding his bike or walking whenever possible, not buying new clothes or shoes, etc.

Every spare penny he earned went towards paying down his home loan. Although this approach seems extreme, he successfully accomplished his goal. If I remember correctly, I believe he paid his house loan off in just 3.5 years! Now, I wanted to mention this story to show how when we are 100%, all-in, dedicated to our goals, amazing things are possible. How badly do we want it? This man had a clear goal with a clear plan to achieve it, plus the consistent actions to make it happen.

Clear goal + Clear plan + Commitment = Completion

Maybe this type of extreme goal is too rigorous for you to consider and implement at this point in your life (or maybe a light bulb just went on), but what could you accomplish if you set your mind to it? The future of your finances is up to you.

Got goals?

I bet you do somewhere in the back of your mind, although maybe you haven't moved intentionally in their direction yet. Or maybe you only have a general sense of *it would be nice someday if...* At least that's a place to start, but chances are high that hopes, dreams and wishes without a plan will never materialize.

Our challenge to you is to put your financial goals and dreams on paper. In our companion workbook called *The Abundance Plan Workbook*, we have a blank page for you to fill in (or copy to a different notebook) with timeframes attached to them. It's called the Financial Goals Worksheet: 20-Year Plan. Filling out this goals worksheet is an important exercise. If you have a spouse or partner, take some time on this. Talk and plan with them. You'll need to be in agreement in order to move in the same direction.

> *"Can two walk together, unless they are agreed?"*
> —Amos 3:3

In 2003, when our oldest child was two and our youngest wasn't even born yet, we had our first financial mentor who had us create our 20-year financial goals. As I'm writing this, I dug through our files and found it. Although it's been stashed away in a file, semi-forgotten, and we haven't looked at it in at least six or seven years, it's surprising how we've kept on track nonetheless! It proves to me that the exercise of talking and discussing, dreaming, strategizing, putting it down on paper, and keeping the goal sheet those many years ago, all by itself, launched us in the right direction.

Just by doing the goal-setting process, it increased the chances we'd reach the goals we established. Did we hit all of them, exactly? Nope. Some still have quite a way to go, but we've accomplished others earlier than expected. I'm very happy with having the target to aim for and at least getting somewhere on the board.

Maybe you feel apprehensive about setting goals. If so, that hesitation may stem from being afraid to fail. It's understandable, because we're taught that failure is bad. Failure means we're stupid. Failure means we never should have tried in the first place. But here's the thing: to not hit a goal should never equal failure. *If I don't set a goal, I won't be disappointed!* Stop thinking that way. It will stunt your life. Our first financial mentor used to say something like, "Why not aim for the stars, and if you only end up hitting the moon, you've done very well."

In my opinion, real failure looks like either:

1. Not setting a goal at all.
2. Setting a goal and doing absolutely nothing to move towards it.

Velleity: the desire, with no intention of doing anything.

Here's some great news though: you have 100% control of both of those. If you set a big goal and get halfway, nice! Good work! If you set a goal that was too easy, hit it and set a new one, higher. Remember the ramen-eating, house-loan payoff guy? He was very dedicated to his goal, and dedication makes all the difference.

Looking back at what's on our 20-year goal sheet, some were too easy and some have proven to be harder than we thought. But have we made progress on those? Yes! We did not fail in those cases, we're still on the path.

Budgets

Once you've set financial goals with timeframes attached to them, one of the first tasks to tackle will be reviewing where your finances are at currently. To get where you want to go, you first have to figure out where you're at now.

"Eight in 10 Americans are broke, and 200 million don't have a budget." –Dave Ramsey

It may not be *the* B-word, but saying "budget" can still cause some eyebrow raising! In simple terms, a budget is making a list and examining income and expenses for a certain period of time (usually per month). A salesperson or real estate agent may ask you, "What is your budget?" What they're really asking is how much is the maximum amount you could spend on a purchase (or on a monthly payment). That's not the type of budget we're talking about now.

The thought of creating a budget may seem daunting for people unfamiliar with financial matters, but it's quite simple. All you need is a piece of paper, a calculator and some numbers: your monthly income, bills and financial account information. In our workbook, we have a blank monthly budget form you can use right now.

Taking control of your money empowers you. You can't get where you want to go without a map, and having a budget on paper is a big part of the map. At its most basic, a budget is just a page (or pages) full of information. But, the information on this helpful little document will tell you how to proceed. Do you need to stop the money bleeding? Are there expenses that could be tightened up a bit? Are you close to paying something off? Is there extra money that can be allocated to something important? Is it time to find creative ways to bring more money into your budget each month? Budgets and goals go hand-in-hand.

> *"A clear vision, backed by definite plans, gives you a tremendous feeling of confidence and personal power."*
> –Brian Tracy, *The Gift of Self-Confidence*

Let's talk about a hypothetical couple's budget.

Sonny and Cher have avoided taking a close look at their finances for a couple years. They're afraid of what they might discover, so it's been easier to ignore budgets, credit scores and balancing their checking account. They have some debt and don't feel financially savvy. When they finally decide to become financially literate and empower themselves, they create a simple spreadsheet budget that looks something like this:

Month/Year ____ / ____	
Monthly Income	**Living Expenses**
Pay/salary:	Grocery/Food:
Tips/bonuses:	Eating out:
Investing income:	Entertainment:
Misc. income:	Beauty:
Giving	Clothing:
Tithe:	Healthcare:
Misc:	Childcare:
Saving	Gas:
Savings account:	Subscriptions:
Investing:	Pet care:
Special savings priority:	Vehicle maint./repair:
Misc:	Other:
Housing	**Debt**
Mortgage/Rent:	Vehicle payment:
Taxes/Insurance:	Vehicle payment:
Home services:	Credit card payment:
Repairs/Maintenance:	Credit card payment:
HOA fee:	Credit card payment:
Furniture:	Personal loan payment:
Appliances:	Student loan payment:
Misc:	Other:
Total monthly income:	*Total monthly payments and expenses:*
$	$
Mo. income minus mo. payments/expenses = **$**	

See The Abundance Plan Workbook for budget worksheets, goals sheets, income ideas and much more.

Although this took a bit of time and mental effort to gather this information, it was a satisfying process for them to finally have the information all in one place. This step was important, since now they can take action on this budget document.

After reviewing it, a few things became clear. First, their income amount is pretty good. Second, they have lingering debt with big monthly payments, taking too much of their income away. Also, they haven't implemented anything to help their money grow. Lastly, there are unnecessary expenses that could be tightened up a bit.

Next Action Steps

Once an individual or couple has completed this budget document, next steps and plans can be formed. That's when the empowerment starts. Depending on what their budget shows and reveals, next action steps for them (and you) might be:

- Formulate a Debt Snowball strategy to pay down debt.
- Figure out a way to bring in more monthly income.
- Determine which expenses could be reduced or eliminated altogether.
- Restructure, consolidate or refinance high interest rate loans.
- Set a dollar amount and save for an emergency fund.
- Set a dollar amount to use/save for investing.
- Plan ahead for known, upcoming expenses.
- Save for a child's college expenses.
- Save for a trip or an upcoming event.

- Make a plan to pay off a home loan.
- Learn about and find new ways to grow and invest surplus savings money.
- Invest in CD's, Roth IRA, savings or municipal bonds, money market funds, 401K, etc.
- Invest money into starting a business that generates more cash flow.
- Invest in real estate, agriculture, metals, whole life insurance plans, dividend-paying stocks, land, etc.
- Start looking at/estimating what retirement expenses might be and create retirement income strategies.

What do you think your next step(s) is?

> *"By failing to prepare, you are preparing to fail."*
> –Benjamin Franklin

Finally, with clarity and data, and a plan in hand, things can change for the better. Your next action steps will help you get closer to achieving the goals you've indicated on your goals worksheet. If you'd like to learn more detailed information about budgeting, we recommend reading Dave Ramsey's *Financial Peace University* information on setting a monthly budget.

Remember the Spending Priority Pyramid? As you set your monthly budget, keep the pyramid in mind. Get rid of worthless spending found on the lowest level and some items from the next level up too, if at all possible. If you find yourself with surplus money in your monthly budget, consider allocating it to your special savings priorities. Your special savings priorities will usually determine your next action steps.

Needed to Live
Necessary Spending
Special Savings Priorities
Not connected to purpose or happiness spending
Not important or worthless spending

"If you don't know where you are going, you'll end up someplace else." –Yogi Berra

Remember when I discussed the people I know who are well-off employees? How they live conservative lives, save money, don't have outlandish spending habits, and know how to do everything a regular financial advisor would recommend? Since we're talking about setting goals for our future, some of you are looking for bigger strategies. You've reached this point in your financial journey:

"I/we have our debts paid off. There's money in savings. Now what?"

Chris and I found ourselves in this spot just before our first child was born. Our cars were paid off, credit cards, furniture loans, and all the other crazy stuff we got ourselves into, and then we had no idea what to do next. The financial advice we had received up to that point seemed lacking for people in our new-found phase. We wanted to steward our money well. We wanted to know what people who have money do with theirs.

Along the way we've found some unexpected knowledge. Maxing out savings accounts, scrimping, 401K's, IRA's, relying on social security, bonds, mutual funds...although this every traditional financial advisor's recommendation, this is not what the ultra-wealthy do with their money. This isn't how they think.

At the risk of seeming contradictory to the budgeting advice just given, I want you to realize something. Budgets are excellent for a majority of people, but aren't vital for everyone.

Think about it. Wealthy families probably don't need to stick to strict monthly budgets. At some point, at some financial level, monthly budgets may not even be relevant anymore. Did these wealthy folks have a time period of financial struggle and need to budget and restrict their spending at some point? Possibly, and if so, it probably helped them get where they are today.

Each one of us needs to recognize where we're at now and take the necessary steps for where we're at, always learning and working towards our next level. Getting to the next level in any area of life requires new wisdom and updated actions.

Someone blew my mind with this question recently: "Are a budget and abundance opposites?" It's definitely food for thought. I can't fully answer that fascinating question yet, but

I suspect budgets need to fit in somewhere along the road to abundance. Maybe living on a budget is a temporary or "seasonal" necessity for those who are on their way to financial independence.

> *"What's the point in trying to get wealthy if it means that you end up living miserably on the way there?"*
> –Mark Ford, author and wealth coach

So, if the ultra-wealthy aren't scrimping, budgeting, socking every penny away into their savings account, or using conventional financial advice fed to the masses by advisors, what *are* they doing? Investing. Let's talk about that next.

Goals Summary

- The exercise of creating goals makes it more likely they will be achieved.
- Clear goal + Clear plan + Commitment = Completion
- Goals and budgets work hand-in-hand.
- Budgeting is very helpful in certain seasons along our financial journey, but strict budgets may not be necessary forever for some people.

Chapter 6

Investing

One of the most important things you can do for your financial life is to get out of bad debt (debt that is a liability and doesn't produce any income). The next key is to invest. You probably hear about investing in the stock market through stock trading, 401Ks, bonds, mutual funds, etc. That is the traditionally peddled advice by Wall Street. But does Wall Street take their own advice?

Interestingly, the word *investing* has been marketed to make people automatically think of putting money into the stock market. The super-rich may have some of their money in the stock market, but mainly they invest in other ways like this:

- Buy investment real estate (using loans/debt, but this debt makes them money)
- Own gold and silver, diamonds and gems (or other precious metals)

- Own businesses, leveraging the work and time of employees and systems
- Invest wisely in opportunities that earn better rates of return than the stock market
- Invest in startup businesses
- Own a business franchise
- Own agricultural land producing yearly harvests
- Offshore banking and currency investing
- Stock options trading
- Own art, historical items and other collectables
- Buy and hold stocks that pay large dividends
- Put their cash in whole life insurance policies rather than in savings accounts

What's the similarity with all of these? They're using their money to make more money, period. They've learned and mastered the art of money multiplication without working more hours. Also notable is the fact that they don't usually do just one of these strategies, alone. Many very wealthy people do several of these at the same time. They diversify. They own rental real estate, gold, dividend stocks, and a business. They own and rent out agricultural land, have a whole life insurance plan, own collectable art, wine and coins, and understand how to safely trade options.

If one area has a downturn, no worries! Because they have a diverse variety of investments, it keeps their wealth safer. And by the way, being "diversified" in the stock market isn't actually diverse. Advisors like to say, "Own stocks and funds in various industries and sectors (manufacturing, medical, financial, metals, technology, communication, etc.) so you can mitigate risk." It seems logical, right? But, when the market tanks, the weight of the crash usually drags nearly everything down at once. Having all of your investment money in the stock market is still having all your eggs in one basket – ask anyone who had a majority of their retirement investment money in the stock market during 2008-2009.

The ultra-rich have lots of baskets. These individuals would rather use the other advanced (and truly diverse) strategies than keep their money in savings accounts earning 1-2% interest. They also want to have more control than the stock market offers on rates of return. Mega-wealthy people don't want most of their retirement money in a 401K or IRA tied to the unpredictable stock market like employees tend to do. Truly wealthy people find ways to get cash flow coming in, all while finding strategies along the way to protect their assets.

Their money makes them money. Money is a seed, growing when planted in the right places. Here's some really good news: you and I can do this, too.

Financial Literacy

In another edition of his newsletter, *Rich Dad Poor Dad Daily*, author and real estate mogul, Robert Kiyosaki advised this to his readers:

Risky:
- *Having no financial education*
- *Blindly turning your money over to a financial planner or adviser*
- *Not understanding the investment and the returns on the*

investment
- *Putting up the majority of the money and the risk and letting others walk away with the majority of the returns*
- *Having no control in your investments*
- *Depending heavily on a financial adviser*

Safe...er:
- *Getting financially educated*
- *Actively investing your money and gaining hands-on experience*
- *Understanding the investment and the returns on the investment*
- *Putting up the majority of the money and the risk and getting the majority of returns*
- *Having control in your investments*
- *Becoming your own financial adviser*

Five things happen to those who don't know how to invest, who do not invest, and who invest poorly.

1. *They work hard all their lives*
2. *They worry about money all their lives*
3. *They depend on others, such as family, a company pension, or the government to take care of them*
4. *The boundaries of their lives are defined by money*
5. *They don't know what true freedom is*

My rich dad said, "You will never know true freedom until you achieve financial freedom." By this he meant that learning to invest is more important than learning a profession. Unfortunately, learning a profession is what most education in our schools is built to do. Our schools are good at training employees but not investors who understand how money works.

Mr. Kiyosaki is convinced that traditional financial advisors and mutual fund managers are only in the business to make money for themselves in commissions, *not* for the financial benefit of you and I. It turns out Wall Street insiders do have money in the stock market...*yours*...that they're earning money on, and then they turn around and use it for more lucrative, higher-return kinds of investments. Interesting how they get their commissions no matter if our accounts make a penny or not for us. If our account loses money, they still get theirs. Hmmm...He makes an intriguing point.

However, for people who have no interest in becoming financially literate for themselves, it's easier to throw money at a 401K, mutual fund or IRA that someone else manages, and hope and pray (when we're 65) they did a good job. That's a risk in itself.

> *"Many backers of the 401(k) now say they have regrets about how their creation turned out despite its emergence as the dominate way most Americans save. Some say it wasn't designed to be a primary retirement tool and acknowledge they used forecasts that were too optimistic to sell the plan in its early days."* –Wall Street Journal

If a 401K was really only designed to supplement a retiree's income, and not be the number one, go-to investment plan for sustaining a retiree throughout their latter years, then why has it become the only answer? It's probably our own fault we're getting gypped. Our lack of financial savvy has left us easy targets. The masses have easily been herded into the automatic, comfortable pen. What you're learning now can empower you to step out of the pen should you choose to do so.

After all, it's your money. I'd like to earn, grow and keep as much of mine as possible, and I suspect you feel the same. By the way, it's interesting how people say *grow* your money. If money is a seed, it grows and produces the best when planted in good soil. More on that thought in a minute.

How to Think Differently

Recently I read this advice about what to look for when investing.

"In Monopoly, players compete by acquiring and developing properties. The one who collects the most rent wins. Usually, that's the person who gets to purchase Boardwalk, because that's the property that provides the highest rent/cash flow. And herein lies one of the crucial principles of value investing...

When you bought Boardwalk, you didn't buy it because of its price. No. You bought it because of the future cash flows you were expecting. Now, apply the same approach to value investing, and you will see that the best metric to use when choosing what to buy [invest in] is price-to-free cash flow."
–Leon Wilfan, Cashflow for Retirement

Our best investment options offer us cash flow in the future (and hopefully even now, too). If we can train our brains to think and ask questions like this, we'll make good investing decisions:

Where can I put my money to work for me? ***Growth.***
Which investments will allow me to put some money into them, and then get more than I put in out of it? ***A profit machine.***
What are "good soil" investments that will keep producing returns and cash flow? ***Continued harvest.***
What can I create or invest in that brings me additional sources of/extra income? ***Multiple streams.***

Get-rich-quick is an idea or mindset based on schemes, and it's a farce. That is not an increase method we support. But, we can get rich over time with investments. Growth of every kind in life is a process – spiritual, physical, emotional, mental, financial. The *big picture*, the *end goal,* always has small steps. Having said that though, accelerated financial growth is certainly possible. Finding legitimate ways to make a lot of money does not have to take 30 years.

"Decisions are like airplanes - you hop on one, and it takes you to a different destination." –Roger Gauthier

Invest for Increase

With money, look for growth opportunities, profit machines, places of continual harvest and/or multiple streams. Increase from investments comes in different forms.

<u>Growth:</u> a trajectory of increase over time, and with basic or low-level maintenance or effort.
Examples: investing in another business or project, dividend stocks, whole life insurance, owning precious metals, owning

and keeping collectables, owning vacant land.

Profit Machine: investment items to buy, hold (short or long-term) and turn for a profit. Some will require effort and special skills; skills and knowledge to improve something and sell it for more.
Examples: rehab property, auction cars or collectables, gold buyer, stock options trading.

Continued Harvest: an investment you buy and hold that continues to give you cash flow many times over, eventually paying back the original investment and more.
Examples: single-family or multi-family home rentals, vacation rentals, commercial real estate leasing, agricultural lands, loans and lending.

Multiple Streams: numerous, various investments and other income-producing activities, large or small, that all generate income and profit.
Examples: side businesses, inventions, authoring books, buying equipment to rent out, renting out a room or an accessory/additional dwelling unit (ADU) on your property, renting out your RV, and hundreds more ideas. See our book called *101 Side Hustles to Make More Money*.

Let's look at each of these increase types even closer.

First, growth. A growth strategy needs to be more than buy, hold and pray. Praying is a really good thing, and we've prayed about investments many times. But, if money is like a seed and we plant it in good soil, the seed has a natural progression, a course, a development, all by itself. It can't help it…that's what it's designed to do. If the seed does what it does automatically, good soil is the key.

> *"And He [Jesus] said, "The kingdom of God is as if a man should scatter seed on the ground, and should sleep by night and rise by day, and the seed should sprout and grow, he himself does not know how. For the earth yields crops by itself: first the blade, then the head, after that the full grain in the head. But when the grain ripens, immediately he puts in the sickle, because the harvest has come."* –Mark 4:26-29

With growth, you're buying and holding an asset of some kind. In some cases the asset doesn't necessarily pay you along the way, but when you sell it, cash it out or take draws from it eventually, you will have more money in your hand than what you started with. Other times you'll get a return along the way, bit by bit. In any case, investing with a focus on growth usually involves strategies that are more *hands-off*.

Maybe you buy and hold a piece of land you think will increase in value in five years (called "land banking"). Maybe you invest in a startup or business that you do not intend on participating in. Maybe you do some options trading and check and adjust your accounts a couple times a week, or buy and hold stocks that pay excellent, quarterly dividends. You could buy and hold gold and silver, waiting lengths of time for metal prices to reach a higher level. Maybe you purchase a collectable item or piece of art, planning to hold it for a while, then sell. In all these scenarios, you're waiting for a value increase. The money you invested is growing without you having to do much along the way.

For profit machines, a very simple example is how pawn

shops operate. They profit from people desperate to sell something, then they turn around to sell it for more. A certain amount of money goes out to buy, and a certain bigger amount comes back when sold. What can you do and invest in to create a profit machine? Will your profit machine look sort of like a business? Maybe. Profit machines are transactions and might involve more participation and time.

My dad is great at finding cars with engine problems, fixing them and reselling. This has become a profit machine for him. It is, in fact, an investment strategy. He is investing money to purchase the cars initially, and gets more out when he sells. It's the same with rehabbing/flipping a home. It's the same with any item of value that can be purchased at one price and sold at a higher price, sometimes (but not always) requiring an improvement, upgrade or update in the middle.

I have a cousin who raises rabbits. He and his wife bought some (invested in rabbits), and they multiplied, literally. He sells the rabbits. Someone else I know grew up with parents who raised and sold goats. My neighbor raises and sells yaks – yep, the big, furry, cattle-like things with horns. Raising animals is also an example of a profit machine, or possibly even the continued harvest method, too.

Continued harvest is next. Aquaponics comes to mind and so does owning real estate: agricultural and rental real estate. The main idea for finding investment options that give you a continued harvest is cash flow. Cash flow keeps coming, monthly, seasonally or whatever.

If you own an investment house, condo, vacation home, apartment building, or commercial property, someone pays you to occupy that property. You receive rent money every month. Sure, you had to pay a down payment to purchase it, and you probably have a loan for the rest. But, think about it: the only money you're "out" is your down payment and your renters will pay off the rest. You get the majority of your asset paid off by someone else, plus at the same time you can fairly confidently expect your asset to appreciate in value over time. The income keeps coming.

Aquaponics and agricultural land are similar – crops are their harvest! Aquaponics uses special water systems and equipment to grow aquatic animals or to cultivate plants and crops. I've known people who have leased out their farmland (for crop or animal use) or have partnered in some way with a farming company, had a sharecropping agreement, etc. In this case, their harvestable asset keeps bringing in money.

Another idea for continued harvest is being someone who lends money. If you're acting as the bank, you can charge interest. I've even heard of investing in independent films, media and movies and earning interest as they pay these loans back. What are some ways you could be earning interest on your money? Better interest rates than pitiful savings account interest, that is…

Multiple streams might go hand-in-hand with any or all of these increase types. You may have heard people talking about multiple streams of income. Imagine rivers and streams for a moment. Some are a peaceful trickle, traveling through a forested area. Some are full of fish and fishermen with hip-waders on, casting out their lines near the opposite shore. Other rivers are massive, dividing countries and sailing ships. They're different sizes, right? Multiple streams of income, no matter the size, add up to more flowing to you.

Can you create something that generates an additional source of income? What can you invest in that creates an additional source of income? Do you have skills or talents that could translate into more income? Take your extra income and invest it into more streams.

Investing Summary

In a nutshell, if we could impart anything to you about investing, it would be these points:

- Invest in assets that make you more money.
- Rich people buy assets that will increase in value (not depreciate) and/or will bring in cash flow.
- The stock market is not your only or greatest option for investing.
- Do your research and due diligence when it comes to investing.
- Investing is not one-size-fits-all. There are many options, so decide what works best for your goals, skills and personality.
- Investing into good soil is key. See our *Spiritual Principles of Money* book.
- You can invest into yourself. Grow yourself in wisdom, spiritual maturity, emotional intelligence and skills. By doing so, you'll almost certainly increase financially.

Chapter 7

Retirement

"How many millionaires do you know who have become wealthy by investing in savings accounts? I rest my case."
–Robert G. Allen

Someday, hopefully, you will retire from working. Here's one thing we know for sure about our retirement years: we'll need money!

Retirement doesn't always mean an absence of work all together, but usually means a transition out of a long-term career or business. Maybe you don't imagine yourself as retired in the traditional sense. Maybe you have a *next thing* plan for your time and energy, such as:

Volunteer work
Managing investments
Hobbies and hobby-related businesses
Side business a few hours a week
Caring for grandchildren
Mentoring others
Be on committees and boards
Traveling

These are some of the valuable things retirees can choose to do with their time. It's nice to have choices; choices that don't come with dire straits about whether or not you can pay your bills or buy necessary medications. Some people wonder if they'll ever be able to retire.

We definitely need money in our retirement years. The big question we all have is *how much*?

As of this writing, according to the U.S. Bureau of Labor Statistics, the average American spends $45,756 per year, or $3,813 per month, in retirement. Relying on Social Security alone comes nowhere near that number.

I recently read about a 2018 report that came out from the Federal Reserve regarding Americans and retirement. They found that 25% of Americans have no retirement plan or pension. This fact didn't surprise me too much. But, combine that with another statistic I heard from the 2018 Retirement Savings survey claiming 42% of Americans have $10,000 or less saved up in accounts for their retirement years. What?! Ten thousand dollars won't get many of us through the next four months, much less the next two decades. A little planning ahead will go a long way.

> *"The average person who thinks even a little about retirement planning ends up with almost twice as much money in retirement as those who reported they didn't think about it at all. It's called the Theory of Planned Behavior, and it states that the pure act of thinking about the future affects our behavior. But, the numbers I am seeing about retirement funding tell me a whole lot of people aren't planning or thinking about it at all."*
> – Steve McDonald, Cashflow for Retirement

It makes me think a lot of people are hoping someone else takes care of them in their retirement years. The government? Their children? For people who have only Social Security to rely on in their later years, I'm not sure how truly secure that is. The Social Security program is the subject of constant political debates and budget-balancing negotiations. It will most likely survive the political wars, but who knows what it will look like in the decades to come. From what I see and the people I know, retirees who struggle the most are the ones who have only government programs to depend on. Having only a Social Security check coming in each month in our retirement years should not be Plan A.

What level of living do you see yourself having? Travel? Same lifestyle as now? Same level of buying power? Or, scaling down? Downsizing everything? Moving to a retirement community? Living with a family member? Senior or assisted living? What you envision and desire for yourself is vital for how you plan.

> *"Always remember that your present situation is not your final destination."* –Zig Ziglar

The question of, "How much disposable income do you want?" comes up often in retirement conversations. *Disposable income*. How I hate that term. While I get the concept—income left after taxes used to save, spend or do whatever with—the words *disposable* and *income* together seem unfitting.

Disposable diapers: something you definitely want to get rid of, fast...
Disposable plates: the "I'm too lazy to wash all this stuff" option...
Disposable gloves: probably used for something gross...

I don't want any of my income to be disposable! All of my

income has an important purpose. Unfortunately, I have a feeling disposable income is a term that is appropriate for some. There's a certain segment of the population that throws their money down some kind of black hole every month. Too bad it isn't being planted like a seed into good soil, like an investment, but rather down some kind of garbage chute, never to be seen again. If that's been your story so far, you can absolutely change it. But, enough of that pet peeve rant...

Finding Your Magic Number

A major concern for some as they approach retirement is, "Will I be able to retire at all?" In 15-18 years, all three of us will be at the traditional retirement age: early to mid-60s. Using the retirement calculators from financial planners or online sites to figure out how much we'll need seems uncertain. What will prices be like then? What will medical care expenses be, knowing politicians can change policies at any time? What will the housing market and prices look like at that time? These are big concerns with no accurate answers. The *magic number* we'll need in a nest egg seems hard to determine accurately. Again, your retirement lifestyle is a huge factor in determining your future income needs.

Here's what we do know for sure. At the most basic level, we will all have these essential expenses our whole lives:

- Housing
- Food
- Clothing and personal care items
- Medical
- Transportation

Housing budgets come with a huge amount of variation, although according to the Bureau of Labor Statistics, the largest expense in retirement is housing (averaging $16,000 a year). What will your retirement housing situation look like? By retirement, will you own your home and have it paid off? Will you own a home with a mortgage payment? Will you rent or lease a home? Will you have a roommate? Will you live with a family member? Will you live in an assisted living or senior living complex? Will you live in an expensive area of the country, a lower-priced area, expensive or low-range neighborhood, or will you live abroad? More on living somewhere else in the world in a minute.

The topic of medical care and coverage during retirement could be a book in itself. Although we aren't Medicare or Medicaid experts, we know there can be significant monthly costs associated with having these government-funded plans. They are not free in most cases. Who knows what costs will be when you and I reach retirement age?

Food prices, clothing and personal care spending also vary quite a bit based on your habits, desires and location.

Transportation will probably be the most predictable category. While gas prices vary some, the price of used cars doesn't that much. I've heard people using this wise plan, and it goes like this: about 3 years before retiring, a person trades in their current car for a semi-new model (new or 2-3 years old with low miles), specifically purchasing the perfect type of vehicle they'll need once they retire. They pay off the newer car before they stop working. It gives them peace of mind in two ways: no more payments and hopefully a newer car equals less maintenance and repair expenses in the coming years.

Again, online sites and financial planners have all kinds of retirement calculators available for you to use. Thinking about the different scenarios we just mentioned will have a huge effect on what your magic number will be.

One of our best pieces of advice is to head into your retirement years with no debt. By eliminating debt and monthly payments, you'll have *much* better peace of mind that your money will stretch adequately. Imagine having no car payments, no mortgage payment and no credit card debt…and no job. That's a much better scenario than having a car payment or two, a mortgage or rent payment and credit card debt…and no job.

> *"Retirement investing is all about creating sustainable passive income. That's because in retirement you need an income stream to cover your costs that doesn't come from a 'normal' job. It's not retirement if you are still working 40+ hours, after all. Perhaps the most straightforward way to generate income - without trading your time for money - is to invest your savings into income-producing securities."*
> –Ben Reynolds, SureDividend.com

Our next best piece of advice is to find ways to keep passive money coming into your budget. Although you may not have a paycheck coming in anymore, you could still have cash flow from other sources. By doing this, once you retire you won't be just draining your savings, IRAs and 401Ks down to nothing for living and medical expenses, wondering if those funds will outlast you or not. Have other investment income rolling in to supplement pensions, 401Ks, IRAs,

Social Security, etc.

What can you invest in today that will keep paying you tomorrow, and next year, and in the next decades to come during your retirement? Put your money to work now rather than putting yourself to work more later. The little old lady or little old man coming after you (future you) will thank you.

International Living?

Most people have never considered the idea of living anywhere else (besides maybe Arizona or Florida) when they retire. Have you ever pictured yourself living outside of the US or Canada? I hadn't until several years ago when one of Chris's previous co-workers retired and moved to Costa Rica. It sounded dreamy.

He sold his house here in the US and his extra belongings, and then bought an ocean-front home on the Pacific Ocean in a small community in Costa Rica. Only the mega-rich can afford these (typically) million dollar plus homes on the beach here in the States. Ocean-front homes in the US are priced out of reach for the majority of households. However, in certain other countries that's often not the case. His retirement accounts, savings and proceeds from his US house sale are stretching further for him in retirement, affording him an even more adventurous experience than during his working years. Why? Because the cost of living is less in his new area, and that's not just exclusive to Costa Rica.

There are dozens of safe countries in Central and South America, Southeast Asia and even in Europe where Canadians and Americans can retire to (or partially retire to) and spend less on food, housing, medical, services, etc.

Ex-pats, as they're called, are people who've relocated themselves to enjoy a lower cost of living and slower-paced lifestyle somewhere else (maybe in the sun). After some study and research, these countries tend to come out on top of the ex-pat living options:

>Panama   Portugal
>Costa Rica   Italy
>Belize   Spain
>Colombia   Thailand
>Uruguay

In terms of safety, infrastructure, medical, cost of living, real estate costs, etc., these countries have proven to be good options for retirees. None of them will be perfect in every way for everyone, but would *you* ever consider this idea? In our resources section, we recommend a couple excellent websites for researching the idea of living abroad.

We're not suggesting all retirees should move away internationally. However, we wanted to throw out the idea so it's at least on your radar. Maybe it doesn't sound appealing to you at all. Maybe you've never thought about it. Maybe it's something you'd like to investigate more!

Whatever your priorities and dreams happen to be, research and plan in that direction. You can start planning in that direction today. We want your retirement years to have great choices available; choices you're excited about and choices you've planned ahead and are ready for.

Retirement Summary

- Retirement looks very different for everyone. For some, it's not a complete absence of work, it's more like *what next?*
- Determine (to the best of your ability) where you'll want to live, what level of lifestyle you desire, type of housing, medical needs, etc., when you are retired.
- Retirement calculators may or may not end up being an accurate picture of how much you'll need per month/year, but at least they can help you start planning.
- Would you consider living outside of the U.S. if it meant a lower cost of living?
- Plan ahead to get rid of debt before you retire.
- Plan ahead to create passive income and cash flow from investments before you retire.

CHAPTER 8

LEGACY

"Someone's sitting in the shade today because someone planted a tree a long time ago." –Warren Buffett

Right now, whether you realize it or not, you're sitting under some kind of tree planted by previous generations. Do you like the tree? Has it been providing you with good things? If not, you can plant a new tree.

What you're doing today, financially and otherwise, has direct implications for your family's future generations. By being purposeful and intentional, you can create a powerful legacy of wisdom, abundance and generosity. In order to leave a legacy, generosity is foundational.

Generous: big-hearted, openhanded, charitable, liberality, plentiful, lavish, giving, unselfishness, abundant. Generosity can be shown with any of our valuable resources – money, time, talents and wisdom.

Part of the legacy each of us has the opportunity to leave is generosity. If we leave the world better than we found it, through our efforts and heart, was it a good life? If we increase good in our communities, families and the world, is that a great legacy? If you are purposeful about planting good trees for the next generation to sit under in the future, was that worthwhile effort? I believe so.

"But a generous man devises generous things, and by generosity he shall stand." –Isaiah 32:8

Notice the fascinating verse above. One word stands out to me: *devises*. To devise something, it means pre-planning and thinking. There's a strategic intentionality involved in devising generous things. The thought of this is exciting. How could you devise generous things and leave (even a small piece of) the world a better place?

Tithing and Giving

Charities, churches, ministries and non-profits often do the work governments cannot. We believe their important, good work deserves support; supporting them by volunteering, sure, but also financially.

In the Bible, God calls His people to tithe on their increase, meaning to give 10% (a tithe/tenth) of wages, crop harvests or any other earnings that equals monetary increase. God directs them to bring the tithe into *His house*; God's house being the storehouse equipped to support community needs.

If you are a church-going person like we are, tithing is essential. It's one of the most basic, fundamental ways we show that we trust in God's faithfulness to provide for us. When we don't give or tithe, there's an underlying mindset of trusting only in ourselves. But, think about this: tithing and giving is a way to tell your money what to do, instead of your money telling you what to do. *Money, go help people. Money, you don't control me. Money, you aren't trustworthy, but God is.* Again, when we support good work, good increases. This leaves a legacy.

Here is another essential idea for devising generous things and leaving the world better than we found it:

Teach Your Kids Money Management Skills and Financial Literacy

You'll change the future by teaching and modeling to your children, grandchildren and other kids who you have the opportunity to mentor about generosity and good stewardship.

As you learn great money habits, you can share them with your children in ways they'll understand, depending on their age(s). In fourth grade, my teacher taught our whole class how to manage a checkbook by each student having a classroom checking account. We earned through efforts, service and just showing up, and had expenditures for various things or penalties for certain offenses. It was brilliant! How can you begin to mentor your children and grandchildren?

> *"Prosperity Literacy: learn about markets, index funds, cryptocurrency, real estate, etc. Become financially literate so you can build a legacy for future generations."*
> –Brian Orme, Pastor

Here are five simple ways you can start teaching your kids (or even other people's kids) about money:

1. Explain money basics at a young age.

When children are very young, the concept of money doesn't fully make sense yet. In Kindergarten, 5-year-olds get basic money lessons on coins and bills at school, but that's about it! With simple explanations, however, they will start to understand and have a picture of how it all works.

Ways to start talking with young children about money can come during many teachable moments. Here are a few conversations you might have:

When I work, I get money to buy things we need…
We need money to buy what we need at the store…
If I buy this, we won't be able to buy that, and that is more important…
When we put money into this bank account, we are saving it up. Then we can use some of that money to take a trip to the beach…
I want to be able to buy you some Christmas presents, so we are not buying this today…
My money is at the bank, and when I use this card, the store takes some of that money out…
If we grow our own food outside, we don't have to spend money on it at the store…
Mommy and Daddy own this house too, but Nancy lives in it. Nancy pays us money to live in our extra house…

Investing and 401K's are obviously over their heads at this early age, but start helping them see how the flow of money happens: income – bank accounts – expenditures – saving. "I make money from my job and it goes into my bank account. When we pay for things, it comes out of my bank account. It's important to save up money for things we may need later."

At every age, talk with them about how you manage your money in ways they will grasp, building on previous lessons, eventually giving them greater insights and some money-management tools to use for themselves.

2. Let them in on your money goals.

Maybe you already have money goals, or you're just starting to create some. Have you already created your 20-year plan? Your kids need to know them. Why? It helps them learn that setting goals is good. It also gets them on board with the household goals.

Maybe you're working on getting out of debt. That's a good discussion. Explain what debt is. Explain what you could have done differently to avoid the debt. Help them see what it's going to take to get rid of it, and the benefits of what life will be like when it's gone.

Maybe you're working on building wealth. Explain what you're doing, why and how. Wealthy families pass along their strategies and methods to the next generation, and sometimes it's the only money and wealth-related teaching people get.

If you deny a child's request to buy them something, explain why. Sometimes mentioning your bigger goal helps them understand.

"Sorry, Honey. Right now we are saving to buy a car/house. That is going to be an amazing day for our family, and we have to be very wise about how we spend until then."

"Sorry, Honey. If I buy this, we may not have enough money saved to go on vacation in the fall. That goal is more important right now."

"Sorry, Honey. This isn't something you really need, and

we're changing the way we spend money."

Be honest with them, even if that means letting them know you've made mistakes with money in the past. Too many parents don't intentionally discuss money with their children, and kids end up learning in indirect, flawed ways such as their perceptions, assumptions or the latest social agendas.

3. Teach them how to earn the things they want.

Now, while it's probably ridiculously harsh to make kids earn their toothpaste or basic school supplies, helping them create their own money goals and strategies to purchase things they'd really like to have is great. It's actually emotionally healthy for children to *not* get everything they've ever wanted and to learn how to earn something. Things earned through effort tend to be more highly valued.

Chris and I taught our two kids about money by creating four envelopes for them:

1. Saving – 30%
2. Spending – 50%
3. Tithe – 10%
4. Others – 10%

With their allowances and other money they earned or received, it was divided up into these four envelopes in certain percentages. The question of, "Mom, will you buy this for me?" was often replied to with, "Do you have any money in your spending envelope?"

We obviously don't want to create money-monster brats, like

a bridezilla who ruins everyone's life until she gets what she wants. Help your children see into their future, having to earn everything they need and want, although they might not like it at first. Although as their parent, you're responsible (for now) for covering their life's needs, start to shift some of the responsibility for their "wants" to them at appropriate ages. They need to understand that someday the purse strings will be cut, and they're on their own.

Will they make good money decisions? Hopefully, so practice with them. "I want an oompa loompa now!" "Forget it, Veruca. Buy your own."

4. Show them household income, expenses, bills, etc.

By sitting down with your kids and showing them what's happening with your accounts, income and bills, you are modeling how to have discussions about money, how to make decisions, how to solve problems and strategize, how to understand budgeting, and eventually how to handle money conversations with their own future kids. You're also opening up communication for them to ask questions, both now and in the future if they need help.

Have them watch you fill in your budget forms. Have them watch you pay bills. Just like you show them how to catch a ball, use the washing machine or bake a cake, they need to be taught these financial life skills, too.

It's okay to be honest with your kids about the current state of your finances. Are they good? Bad? Ugly? Talk about your learning curve. Talk about what you wished you had learned growing up or about helpful money tips you did learn. It's okay for them to know you don't have all the answers, but that you're learning and growing now.

5. Discuss money mindset and money as a tool.

As your kids mature, talk about the power of money – how to earn it and use it wisely, but also how to *not* allow it to rule them. Money is a fantastic tool, but a terrible master. Let them know that money is important, although it shouldn't be their life's number one focus. Too many people jump into an education path or career because of the earning potential alone, not considering if it's really their calling or if it uses their gifts and talents...or if they'll even really enjoy it. Explain how just *following the money* and forgetting purpose and happiness can cause a person to end up rich, yet sad, wondering if their life has any meaning or significance.

> *"A wise person should have money in their head, but not in their heart."* –Jonathan Swift

Give them a picture of what financial stability looks like vs. financial instability. "Which one do you want when you grow up?" Help them see what's possible if they steward their money well, and help them recognize what consequences will happen if not. Money can get them where they want to go in life, but can devastate their dreams if mismanaged. Point out examples as you come across them in your daily life. Answer their curious questions. Kids notice more than we realize.

"Dad, why do the Andersons have a lot of money?"
"Well, they have made some great decisions. They have well-paying jobs because of education and skills they've

developed, plus they decided to invest in real estate a while back. They have income from work and investments, both. They also spend wisely."

"Mom, why can't Aunt Teresa ever go with us on vacation?" "Unfortunately, she has too many bills to pay. She doesn't have any extra money now because she's still trying to pay back the money she spent with her credit cards and other loans. I wish she could come with us, but she hasn't planned ahead."

"Do you see this credit card offer we got in the mail? It has a 19% interest rate, which is crazy high. If we bought stuff at the store with it and didn't pay the bill off every month, we'd be stuck paying off the same stuff for years. Credit cards only work well for people if they're able to pay the whole amount off each month when the bill comes."

Discuss their observations – what choices went well and what went wrong helps them analyze situations they might someday find themselves in, and will hopefully help them make financially intelligent decisions later on. *Hmm...I don't want that for myself...how can I avoid that? I want my life to look like that...what does it take to get there?*

Our choices, mindset, habits and the information we have access to are all that separates each of us from each other. Otherwise we all have the same 24 hours a day to work with. As you learn and become more financially literate, gaining new strategies and knowledge, teach your children, too. Help your children see into the future – to see the big picture. Talk with them about things like this:

- The money mindset of your future spouse is a huge consideration.
- There are kids who have started successful businesses. Why not you?
- Get the advice of people who are where you want to be.
- Even if you think you're not good at math in school, at least gain a solid understanding of consumer math and finances. Financial math is much easier to understand than algebra and geometry.
- Someday you'll have a career or own your own business, doing work that helps people in some way.
- Someday you'll have a family and home you're taking care of.
- Someday you'll be making decisions on how and where to invest your money.
- What kind of financial situation do you desire for yourself? What will it take to have that?

Give your children a picture of the choices and opportunities in store for them and get them thinking about it. Right now you're learning, and we applaud you for doing so. Next, it will be your turn to educate your kids. When young people don't learn about money at an early age, before their money responsibilities start, they may have years of needless struggle (like many of us have experienced).

"Give me six hours to chop down a tree and I will spend the first four sharpening the axe." –Abraham Lincoln

Young People...

If you're a young person reading this right now, just getting started in your financial life, debt avoidance is one of our biggest keys for you. Starting out on the right foot will set your financial life up for success, but we realize many people aren't learning valuable financial lessons early enough in life.

If we could recommend a few critical things to young people, it would be these:

- Debt avoidance – avoid going into (bad, unproductive) debt (credit cards, cars, etc.).
- Living within your means – not spending more than you earn. Stay within your pay, which typically is low when you're young.
- Find work you're passionate about and get the education you know you'll use for sure. Avoid student loans when possible.
- Don't go hog wild with spending as a young adult in your new-found freedom (although it's tempting to)!
- Learn more money wisdom and advanced strategies about wealth-building (beyond being a good employee and socking money away in a savings account).

If you're 35 or 55, of course these pieces of advice still apply! But often at 35 or 55, we wish we'd known (and done) these things much earlier in life. Just today on the radio I heard the DJ lamenting about debt, and she said, "What were you thinking, 20-something me?"

> *"The best time to plant a tree was 20 years ago. The second-best time is now."* Chinese Proverb

Along with debt avoidance, another big key is to find ways to wisely invest early. When it comes to investing, the earlier the better, but better late than never. Keep in mind that investing in yourself—in education, personal and spiritual development, honing your skills, developing gifts and talents—brings a great return on investment (ROI). *You* are good soil to sow and invest into. Gaining wisdom always pays off.

What About Kids and College?

This is a side note for parents of college-aged young adults and older teens. All of us want to see our children do well in life. We have hopes for them; hopes they'll go to college or get specialized training of some kind and go on to change the world. If we're able to pay for our child's college education, fantastic. If we aren't able to, and financial aid or scholarships aren't covering the bulk of their education expenses, we may be putting our child's financial future in jeopardy.

This advice may be controversial, but we hope it sparks conversations.

If your child's only chance for higher learning is becoming burdened for the next decade (or often a lot longer) with large student loans, proceed carefully – especially if they're wishy-washy about going to college in the first place, are undecided about what their major or career should be, or are generally unmotivated about work and school. If they're driven, ambitious, decided, passionate, and eager to study hard for a particular career they'll love and pays well, then have at it. Coming out of college with student loans may be a necessary evil.

However, I've seen way too many young adults and even people in their 40s and 50s with student loan debt still hanging over their heads, in careers and jobs they never went to school for. "But if they don't go directly from high school into college, will they ever get their degree?" That thought lingers in many of our minds, and it's a valid concern.

There are other non-traditional ways people make money and build happy lives. There are ways to pay for higher education, quarter by quarter, alongside of working. Just some food for thought. We're definitely not advocating for skipping higher education. Higher education is a wonderful legacy. Student loan debt for decades, however, is not. Proceed with student loans cautiously.

Have Honest Conversations

I've heard well-meaning, loving parents say something like: "I'll do whatever it takes to see my child through college, even if it means taking all the equity out of my house." At the risk of shipwrecking their own finances and retirement, some parents believe this is what's expected of them. It's noble, but ill-advised. Your job as a parent is to do your best to set your children up for success, but it isn't necessarily to finance it all. Remember, you still have goals and necessities for your own financial future to take into account.

If you have very young children, look into starting a 529 college savings account for them. According to nerdwallet.com, "529 college savings plans are the most common type [of account to save for college expenses]. Investments grow tax-free and can be withdrawn tax-free for educational expenses like tuition, room and board, and required textbooks. 529 prepaid plans let you prepay part or all of an in-state public tuition, locking in the tuition at time of payment." Start saving with a 529 plan now and you may not be faced with a dilemma when they reach age 18.

Another well-meaning, loving parent may have this opinion: "You must get a degree, whatever it takes, even if it means loans." There are clear downsides to starting out an adult life deep in debt. There are also benefits to starting out an adult life with a degree. Some families place high value on every family member getting a college degree, which is commendable.

I've also heard other well-meaning, loving parents say, "I can offer you this much $__ to help you with college, and I can help you locate scholarships to apply for. The rest will be up to you."

None of these are wrong. None of these are the only way it should be done. What will be best for your family?

In my family (Krista), my parents were divorced. The agreement was that my father would pay 1/3 of my college costs, my mother 1/3 and me 1/3. I got an AA degree after high school and started working at a real estate office shortly thereafter. After working for several years and getting married, I went back for an additional two years of college, paying for it myself with money from my full-time work.

In Chris's experience, he had to pay for college himself, but was able to live at home for free. He went to a local community college for his first two years, and a nearby university for the last two years. He worked at a department store during this time, earning commission on electronics sales, paid his college expenses as he went, and came out of college with just a $2500 loan left to pay.

When our children were born, we set up college savings accounts for each of them similar to 529 plans. We saved up and have pre-paid for two years of their university-level education, bit by bit over many years. As they grew, we let them know that two of their four years was paid for and the other two years would be up to them.

Thankfully, Washington State has what's called Running Start – a program for high school juniors and seniors to attend classes at a local community college, earning an AA degree and their high school diploma simultaneously. It's nearly free – approx. $350 per quarter. Brilliant! Right now our oldest is taking advantage of this program, so with this decision, he will have no college expenses to pay for himself to earn his bachelor's degree. Our youngest plans to do the same. Does your state offer the same opportunity?

Chris and Kayla (Chris' daughter) had a very different scenario. As a teen, Chris received scholarships and grants during her first two years at a community college and finished her AA Degree with zero debt. She then went to a private college and had to take out student loans to do her third year at school. She ended up dropping out and had to pay on those student loans for over six years.

Kayla also received scholarships and grants for her first two years. Chris also used Washington State's GET program over the years to help save up for Kayla's college expenses. During Kayla's first two years, Chris was able to pay cash for whatever cost was not covered by grants, scholarships and the GET money. Kayla left the community college with zero debt and an AA degree.

Kayla then went on to a four-year college and lived in an apartment with a roommate. Kayla received some grant money from the college for the first year, but during her second year, Chris also decided to finish her four-year degree! Between Kayla and Chris simultaneously finishing their degrees, four loans were taken out, totaling about $24,000. Not bad for both of them tackling college-level studies at the same time! Chris and Kayla have already paid off two of the loans, in less than two years. Chris says, "While it was not ideal, we both finished our degrees and have a much higher earning capacity now. I'm still glad we did it."

There's no right or wrong, just choices, and every choice has its pros and cons. The planning involved for college or higher-learning expenses is as unique as each family themselves. In any case, start planning for expenses as soon as possible. Start the discussion with your child at least by the time they reach high school. Figure out what is going to work out and be the most beneficial for everyone; for your student and for you. Getting a college-level education can be part of a family's legacy, but so can be being debt-free after higher learning.

More Legacy

Leaving a legacy through teaching your children, grandchildren, nieces or nephews is amazing. You may have heard the term *generational wealth*. It starts with you, then continues. In a book we read called *What Would the Rockefellers Do?*, we learned a strategy wealthy families use to retain and foster generational wealth.

You've probably heard of the Rockefeller family. They were tycoons responsible for building banks, holding large amounts of real estate and running companies in the oil industry back in the mid to late 1800's. John D. Rockefeller was the world's first billionaire. Apparently, the Rockefellers are still in the top 50 richest families in America today, 160+ years later. Not the Vanderbilts though. The mega wealth the Vanderbilt family created through their shipping and railroad empire during the same era was all but gone three generations later. Millions, *gone.*

There are many facets to the Rockefellers' generational success, but it turns out the family implemented one specific thing that has made a big difference: whole life insurance policies for each family member. We don't sell insurance and don't claim to have all the information on how these whole life insurance policies work, but we wanted to share the idea so you can investigate it more. Using these policies, family members can borrow from the family fortune rather than banks, save money within these policies like savings accounts (but with much larger rates of return compared to savings accounts), and are guaranteed a large death-benefit payout amount to their heirs upon death. We'd recommend looking into these whole life insurance policies further.

> *"A good person leaves an inheritance for their children's children, but a sinner's wealth is stored up for the righteous."* –Proverbs 13:22

Of course, opportunities abound to leave money to organizations, churches, ministries, PBS TV, local outreach services, and other valuable charities and groups in your will. Doing so is a great idea for leaving a legacy. Passing your wisdom along is also a form of generosity, and generosity is the foundation of leaving a legacy. Again, the question we can ask ourselves:

> *What generous things could I devise in order to leave (even a small piece of) the world a better place?*

If money, time, talents and wisdom are our main resources, there are a lot of options for us. For our purposes here, we hope to help you increase financially; increase in order to benefit yourself, obviously, but also others. I'm sure we can all agree that the generosity others have shown us is often what has made the world a sweeter place.

> *"If you're going to live, leave a legacy. Leave a mark on the world that can't be erased."* –Maya Angelou

Legacy Summary

- What we do today affects our future and the future of others (especially those in our family).
- Share your financial knowledge with the next generation.
- Higher education costs are a topic each family should openly discuss to sort out the pros and cons of the multiple options available.
- In all that we do with our money, our goal should be to leave the world a better place.

Conclusion

"It is not real estate, stocks, mutual funds, businesses, or money that makes a person rich. It is information, knowledge, wisdom, and know-how—a.k.a. financial intelligence—that makes one wealthy." –Robert Kiyosaki

As you've probably noticed, our financial mindset and methods are slightly different than what you may hear from other sources. We're not selling financial products, loans or accounts. We don't own a bank, so we don't have any benefit from you keeping a bunch of money in a savings account or taking out loans. We aren't financial planners working for a major financial company, so we aren't steering you towards opening more IRAs or mutual fund accounts. The advice and ideas in our books and mentoring groups have no reward or self-serving gain to direct you to this or that service.

Our goal is simply to help you make the most of your money through good stewardship, proper mindset, creative strategies, and setting *good* goals. *Good* goals, meaning one's best goals include good things coming to themselves and their family as well as to see the good things of this world increase. How can your goals be good for you and also cause more good to flourish around you?

We want to see you get ahead. Why would we do this? Why would we bother with all the work involved for SaveMoneyandBuildWealth.com and The Abundance Plan? We're not exactly sure, really, other than God must have us on a mission. The life lessons along our journeys are what we can turn and now share with you.

Poverty sucks. Deep down it's disturbing for us to watch families struggle. It's perturbing to see people get sucked into bad money deals and bad habits. Knowing people aren't learning about money, weren't modeled good spending habits, don't have useable information about investing, aren't sure how to steward money well when they have some, keep old, unhelpful mindsets, aren't aware of how side hustles can bring more money into their budgets, haven't learned tactics on how to stretch their money further…all of it…drives us to teach. It also drives us to continue learning for ourselves.

Your financial breakthrough could be just one new thought and habit away.

As we conclude this book, we realize your success with money hinges on this one factor:

Will you actually make a change to your habits?

And, typically habits change second, following a mindset change. But, let me be clear, a mindset shift alone won't get the job done. *Nothing* will actually change in your money and financial situation if your habits and your actions don't change.

Learning is amazing and can be fun. However, don't be like one of my cousins who went to college for ten years with no clear goal. A mature person turns their learning into action, so take what you've learned and the understanding you now have and go do something amazing with it. Make some changes and adjustments where needed. When a huge change is needed, start by making changes one by one to make it more manageable.

"Unless commitment is made, there are only promises and hopes; but no plans." –Peter F. Drucker

We are praying for your financial wisdom and increase.

May God richly bless you in every area of life,
Chris, Krista and Chris

To continue learning about money mindset, ideas and strategies, sign up to receive our e-newsletter and read our other books in this series:

Spiritual Principles of Money
101 Ways to Stretch a Dollar
101 Side Hustles to Make More Money
Save Money by DIY'ing Just About Anything
The Abundance Plan Workbook

Join our Facebook group:
www.facebook.com/groups/savemoneyandbuildwealth/
Sign up for our e-newsletter: Abundant Living News
Follow us on Instagram: @savemoneyandbuildwealth

Resources Section

Recommended Books:
How Heaven Invades Your Finances by Jim Baker
Money Mysteries from the Master by Gary Keesee
Cash Flow Quadrants by Robert Kiyosaki
Financial Peace University by Dave Ramsey (for budgeting and Debt Snowball)
Retired and Free by Pedro Adao
What Would the Rockefellers Do? by Garrett Gunderson

Living Abroad:
www.LiveandInvestOverseas.com
www.InternationalLiving.com

Whole Life Insurance Information and Sales:
Fortress Financial and Insurance Services
https://www.fortressfg.com/optin16571883

Develop Entrepreneurial and Financial Skills:
100X Academy coaching - **https://bit.ly/2EO4dTb**

Article about student loan forgiveness:
https://bit.ly/2YskPGG

Ideas to make $$ while you sleep:
https://bit.ly/2WpK7Fw

About the Author

Krista Dunk is an author, speaker, real estate investor, and the project director for two book publishing companies. Krista has written several books. Her first book, *Step Out and Take Your Place*, published in 2011, helps people of God discover their God-given gifts and calling by taking a journey to seek Him. She has also published a devotional, the Ninja Kitty children's book series, as well as books in The Abundance Plan book series.

As a child and young adult who struggled with timidity, Krista now finds herself speaking and training in front of audiences large and small. She is passionate about helping people get a vision for how their life could look and to step out into it.

Krista and Chris, her husband of 26+ years, live in Washington State with their two teenagers. Krista, Chris and their friend, Chris Creekpaum, make up the Save Money and Build Wealth training team.

Learn more at:
www.KristaDunk.com
www.SaveMoneyandBuildWealth.com

Speaking and Training

Interested in speakers for your group, event, conference, church, or online training on faith and finance topics? Looking to host a special workshop or need small group curriculum to help people save money and build wealth?

Connect with the Save Money and Build Wealth team today – Chris, Krista and Chris! This power trio is fun, experienced and loves to help others get breakthrough in the area of money and finances. They are also dedicated to helping people get new, biblically-based mindsets that will give them freedom in many areas of their lives.

Money-Related Training Topic Examples:
101 Ways to Make More Money
101 Ways to Stretch a Dollar
The 5 Uses of Money
Financial Goal Setting
Teen and Young Adult Money Success Kickstart
Stewarding Money God's Way
Money Mindset for Abundance
Discovering Your Money Journey's Next Step

Connect with our team today at
TheAbundancePlan@gmail.com
or on our Facebook group page at
www.facebook.com/groups/savemoneyandbuildwealth

The Abundance Plan Book Series:
Available Now:

<u>Coming soon:</u>
Save Money by DIY'ing Just About Anything
101 Ways to Stretch a Dollar
101 Side Hustles to Make More Money

Exclusive Publishing for Kingdom Entrepreneurs
www.100Xacademy.com

www.ingramcontent.com/pod-product-compliance
Lightning Source LLC
Chambersburg PA
CBHW070655220526
45466CB00001B/447